AF251342

A TOUR

THROUGH THE
SOUTHERN AND WESTERN TERRITORIES
OF THE

UNITED STATES

OF

NORTH-AMERICA;

By JOHN POPE.

A FACSIMILE REPRODUCTION
OF THE 1792 EDITION, WITH AN
INTRODUCTION AND INDEXES
BY *J. Barton Starr.*

BICENTENNIAL FLORIDIANA
FACSIMILE SERIES.

A University of Florida Book

University Presses of Florida
Gainesville   1979.

THE BICENTENNIAL FLORIDIANA
FACSIMILE SERIES
published under the sponsorship of the
BICENTENNIAL COMMISSION
OF FLORIDA,
SAMUEL PROCTOR, *General Editor.*

A FACSIMILE REPRODUCTION
OF THE 1792 EDITION
WITH PREFATORY MATERIAL, INTRODUCTION,
AND INDEXES ADDED.

PRINTED IN FLORIDA
BY STORTER PRINTING COMPANY,
GAINESVILLE.

Library of Congress Cataloging in Publication Data

Pope, John.
  A tour through the southern and western territories
of the United States of North-America.

    (Bicentennial Floridiana facsimile series)
    "A University of Florida book."
    Photoreprint of the ed. printed by J. Dixon, Richmond.
    Includes bibliographical references.
    1. Southern States—Description and travel. 2. Ohio
Valley—Description and travel. 3. Southwest, Old—
Description and travel. 4. Creek Indians. 5. Pope,
John. I. Title. II. Series.
[F213.P82 1979]   917.3   78–26408
ISBN 0–8130–0418–7

BICENTENNIAL COMMISSION OF FLORIDA.

Governor Reubin O'D. Askew, *Honorary Chairman*
Lieutenant Governor J. H. Williams, *Chairman*
Harold W. Stayman, Jr., *Vice Chairman*
William R. Adams, *Executive Director*

Dick J. Batchelor, Orlando
Johnnie Ruth Clarke, St. Petersburg
A. H. "Gus" Craig, St. Augustine
James J. Gardener, Fort Lauderdale
Jim Glisson, Tavares
Mattox Hair, Jacksonville
Thomas L. Hazouri, Jacksonville
Ney C. Landrum, Tallahassee
Mrs. Raymond Mason, Jacksonville
Carl C. Mertins, Jr., Pensacola
Charles E. Perry, Miami
W. E. Potter, Orlando
F. Blair Reeves, Gainesville
Richard R. Renick, Coral Gables
Jane W. Robinson, Cocoa
Mrs. Robert L. Shevin, Tallahassee
Don Shoemaker, Miami
Mary L. Singleton, Jacksonville
Bruce A. Smathers, Tallahassee
Alan Trask, Fort Meade
Edward J. Trombetta, Tallahassee
Ralph D. Turlington, Tallahassee
William S. Turnbull, Orlando
Robert Williams, Tallahassee
Lori Wilson, Merritt Island

GENERAL EDITOR'S PREFACE.

MANY Americans after the Revolution were curious about the western and southern lands ceded by Britain to the United States in the Paris peace agreement of 1783. Only a handful of travelers had journeyed through this area, and little was known of the land or of the peoples who lived there. Most Americans satisfied their curiosity by reading the few published travel accounts of the more adventuresome, or the more reckless, of their fellow citizens, who were willing to take a chance of being murdered by an Indian, gored or eaten by a wild beast, or taken captive by some unknown enemy.

One of those who traveled in 1783 and 1784 into "the southern territories" of East Florida was a German named Johann David Schoepf. He published an account of his journey in a volume entitled *Travels in the Confederation*. Schoepf sailed south from Charleston and along the coast of Georgia to St. Augustine. There he lodged with a German baker and his wife and explored the surrounding countryside. Schoepf describes the vegetation, climate, animal life, the people, their houses and churches. This valuable and insightful account, written in German, was translated and published in the United States in 1911.

Of more importance is the travel journal of Colonel John Pope of Virginia who toured the "Southern and Western Territories of the United States" in 1790. The good colonel is an enigma about whom very little is known. Some historians have wondered if he ever existed at all and if his travel account is not a work of fiction. Professor J. Barton Starr, who has edited Pope's *Tour of the Southern and Western Territories of the United States* for the Bicentennial Floridiana Facsimile Series, has established that John Pope was a real person and that his "tour" did indeed take place. Pope began his peregrinations the year following the adoption of the new constitution in Philadelphia. In Europe, the French Revolution was sending forth shock waves to every part of the continent. These events in Philadelphia and in Europe would change the world, but Colonel Pope seemed little aware of them; he makes no mention of these stirring episodes in his travel account.

America was moving in 1790, and Manifest Destiny was fast becoming an American passion. There was no limit to how far the country's boundaries would eventually be extended, many of its citizens believed. First, however, the newly acquired lands would have to be "examined," and this was the role played by men like John Pope.

Pope started his journey from Richmond on June 1, 1790, and four months later he had reached Pittsburgh. Turning south to Louisville, he then proceeded down the Ohio and Mississippi rivers to New Orleans. From there he journeyed to West Florida. His visit to Pensacola provides important historical information on the city, its people, and their business activities, particularly the trading firm of Panton, Leslie and Company. After stopping with Alexander McGillivray, the half-breed chief of the Creeks, Pope traveled through Georgia to Augusta. He tried to get into East Florida, but when the Spanish refused to allow his ship to enter the St. Johns River, he put in at St. Marys, Georgia. From there he returned North, ending his long sixteen-month tour in Philadelphia.

Colonel Pope published his travel account in 1792. How popular the book was, no one can now ascertain, but it has become over the years a very rare volume. J. Barton Starr, the editor of this facsimile volume, which is published by the University of Florida Press for the American Revolution Bicentennial Commission of Florida, is a member of the history faculty at Troy State University at Fort Rucker, Alabama. A native of Pensacola, Dr. Starr is a graduate of Samford

University and Florida State University. His publications include two books: *Tories, Dons, and Rebels: the American Revolution in British West Florida, 1775-1783* (Gainesville, 1976) and *Alabama: A Place, People, a Point of View* (Dubuque, Iowa, 1977). He is also the author of a monograph, *To Live (and Die) in Dixie* (Troy, Alabama, 1978). His scholarly articles have been published in the *Florida Historical Quarterly*, the *Alabama Review*, and the *Alabama Historical Quarterly*, and he has delivered papers at a number of professional meetings and conferences. He is the recipient of a Fulbright-Hays Senior Lectureship to spend a year in Hong Kong.

SAMUEL PROCTOR.
General Editor of the
BICENTENNIAL FLORIDIANA
FACSIMILE SERIES.

INTRODUCTION.

HE was never born, lived only two years, wrote his travel account from a comfortable chair in Richmond, and never died. After roughly six months of intensive research involving nearly as much travel as is contained in the book under investigation, I had just about reached this conclusion concerning Colonel John Pope. In the course of my research for this introduction, I discovered that numerous other historians had attempted to unearth Pope, only to give up in frustration. Such a challenge made me even more determined to locate the pertinent material. After doing research in fifteen different depositories and corresponding with approximately thirty-five others, I must regrettably now take my place among the confounded, but not among the conquered. Colonel Pope and his travel account proved as elusive as the proverbial pot of gold at the end of the rainbow. I have, however, through persistence (perhaps stubbornness is a better word) and pure luck, been able to verify the existence of Pope and the authenticity of his travel account. In so doing, I have developed a profound admiration for a man who could make the exhausting trip of several thousand miles, remain lucid enough to write a useful record of that trip, and at the same time visit with over sixty people—including many prominent people such as George Rogers Clark, General Adam Stephen, Senator Pierce Butler, Hugh Henry Brackenridge, General Horatio Gates, Governor Manuel Gayoso de Lemós, Commandant Carlos de Grand-Pré, Joseph Habersham, Alexander McGillivray, Daniel Morgan, Governor Arturo O'Neill, Governor Edward Telfair, Charles Washington, Secretary of War Henry Knox, and Colonel Isaac Zane—and manage to be mentioned in the papers of only two of them. Pope apparently then returned to Richmond to publish his book where his only legacy is a handwritten note on the last sheet of the University of Virginia's copy of his magnum opus: "Pope you are a damned fool."

But Colonel John Pope's *Tour through the Southern and Western Territories of the United States of North-America* . . . is an entertaining book of some importance. While "Mere Occurencies, and the most conspicuous Traits of Men and Manners, are the principal objects of my Investigation,"[1] Pope's observations—occasionally quite florid and fanciful—are basically accurate.

He commits an occasional error, but it is unintentional, as his aim was to present an accurate account of his tour as he perceived it. But who was Colonel John Pope, and why did he make the extensive journey?

———

"Almost nothing is known about the author"; "extended search has brought to light little concerning him"; "you ask the million-dollar question . . . respecting biographical data on John Pope"; such is the secondary evidence concerning the baffling Pope.[2] Virtually nothing has come to light concerning Pope's early life, but from textual evidence (page 79), Pope lived in Amherst County, Virginia, at the time of the American Revolution. The text (page 9) also clearly indicates that he served as an officer during that conflict. While there are several John Popes from Virginia listed as having served in the Revolution,[3] the evidence is conclusive that John Pope, Jr., of Amherst County was recommended as a major in the militia in June 1780, and in May 1781, "John Pope Jr. Gent." was recommended as a lieutenant colonel of the first battalion of the militia. A month later he qualified as lieutenant colonel. While there is no clear service record for Pope, his battalion saw duty at Lynch's Ferry, Cowpens, Rockfish Gap, and the Battle of Jamestown, and joined the "Main

Army under Gen. Lafayette & other generals" for the Battle of Yorktown.[4]

After Yorktown, Pope apparently returned to Amherst County where he was listed as residing in the 1783 and 1785 censuses.[5] As a militia officer and styled a "Gent.," Pope undoubtedly was in the upper level of Amherst County society and took his community responsibilities seriously, for in May 1782, he was appointed "Surveyor of the Road."[6] Little else is known of Pope during this period, although as late as 1785 he was listed in the Amherst County Personal Property Book, and in 1791 he was shown in the Land Tax Books for the same county as holding 719 acres. Page 52 of the text of Pope's *Tour* clearly implies that he was residing in the area of Richmond and Manchester by 1790. The land records for Amherst County verify that in 1790 Pope sold all of his land to William Duval.[7] While he indicates that he moved to the Richmond and Manchester area of Virginia, there is nothing in the records of Chesterfield County or Richmond City to indicate such a fact. There is a John Pope listed in the Land Tax Books for 1787–1790, and in the Personal Property Books from 1786 through the early nineteenth century in Richmond County on the Northern Neck of Virginia.[8] There is, however, nothing to definitely authenticate that this is our Colonel Pope. Pope was a common name in late-eighteenth-century Virginia, and there are a number of "John Popes" listed in contemporary records. The only safe conclusion is that Colonel Pope lived in Amherst County until around 1790 when he moved to the neighborhood of Richmond and Manchester, whence he began his tour.

———

That Pope moved appears obvious, that he made a tour is certain, but why he made the trip is open to question. The most obvious explanation for the trek through the American wilderness is intellectual curiosity and a desire for excitement. Apparently well-educated, as evidenced by his writing ability, his occasional use of Latin, and his frequent quoting from such diverse sources as Milton, Voltaire, Dryden, Samuel Butler, Aristotle, Robert Burton, and Alexander Pope, the prospect of mental stimulation must have had a strong appeal to Pope. On the other hand, after the excitement of watching "the world turned upside down," the gentry life of Amherst County might have been dull to the Revolutionary War officer. The certainty of new adventure undoubtedly attracted Pope. Or it may well have been, as former President Theodore Roosevelt would put it over a hundred years later, it was his "last chance to be a boy."

Whatever personal reasons Pope may have had for his tour, there apparently was also a very practical reason for the journey. In a later meeting with Secretary of War Henry Knox, Pope informed the secretary that he had undertaken the trip as an agent of Patrick Henry and David Ross of the Virginia Yazoo Company.[9] By the time Pope traveled to the western regions of Georgia, Patrick Henry's land speculation company had been granted over seven million acres of land on the Tennessee River for $93,741, and it is therefore possible that Pope made the tour on business connected with the company. There is, however, nothing in the major collections of Patrick Henry's papers to indicate that he even knew John Pope, much less that the traveler served as his agent. In addition, Pope's *Tour* is not concerned with land and prospects for future development but is instead a hodgepodge of general observations. While it is possible that Pope served as a representative for the Virginia Yazoo Company and made a second report, there is nothing to verify this, and it is unlikely that such a trip would have completely escaped Henry's correspondence.[10]

Whatever the motivation for the journey, Colonel John Pope left Richmond on June 1, 1790, on a trip that would carry him through populous cities and small villages, across rampaging rivers and quiet streams, and into Indian country and hostile Spanish territory. Not knowing what lay ahead, Pope would venture into the unknown for sixteen months before ending his journey in the nation's temporary capital at Philadelphia. Constantly plagued by rheumatism, colds, snakebite, and various other illnesses, as well as by horse thieves and occasionally hostile Indians and Spaniards, the colonel's venture is remarkable for the late eighteenth century. While other travelers wrote more detailed or more colorful accounts than John Pope, few adventurers of the period could match his endurance. The sheer distance involved makes Pope's expedition one of the outstanding accomplishments of the last quarter of the eighteenth century.

After leaving Richmond, Pope quickly passed through Virginia to Winchester, where he remained several days. While there he visited with General Daniel Morgan and had his horse stolen by a former soldier in his regiment. From Winchester he journeyed through Berkeley County, Shepherd's Town, and Martinsburg, Virginia, on his way to Redstone on the Monongahela River. Along the way he met with Charles Washington, General Horatio Gates, and General Adam Stephen. Forced to remain for a week at Redstone—the usual gathering place for expeditions down the Monongahela—Pope finally reached Pittsburgh in October 1790. Remaining in the city for ten days because of illness, Pope here met the "celebrated" Hugh Henry Brackenridge. Enthralled with Brackenridge's recent marriage to Miss Sabina Wolfe, author Pope wrote a poem to Brackenridge "on his being fairly Noos'd." Pope reports that Brackenridge published the poem in the Pittsburgh *Gazette*, but unfortunately this journal is not extant for the last six months of 1790. The poem is included in Pope's *Tour* and is an example of the type of poetry Pope frequently wrote and included in his work. He is "little noted nor long remembered" for his poetry.[11]

Colonel Pope departed Pittsburgh in November 1790 for the long journey down the Ohio and Mississippi rivers to New Orleans. Passing through Limestone and Danville, Kentucky, he arrived at Louisville in December to visit General George Rogers Clark. Fearing that the general "hath actually been in a profound Slumber of upwards of four Years, without the least Symptoms of Wakefulness whatever," Pope was undoubtedly pleased to find that Clark "immediately recognized me." Pope also commented on the "southern hospitality" of the people of Louisville: "for such is the extreme Hospitality of the People, that unknown to their Guest, they will confer, or rather impose Acts of Beneficence, which cannot be refused without Rudeness."

On March 4, 1791, Pope began the longest leg of his journey, leaving Louisville for his trip down the Ohio and Mississippi to New Orleans and the Gulf of Mexico. Briefly stopping at New Madrid (or Greasy Bend), where he dined with the Spanish commandant Pedro Foucher, Pope proceeded down the Mississippi to Natchez. Before reaching that community, however, his party encountered Louisiana Governor Manuel Gayoso de Lemós, who entertained him aboard the governor's "barge." Pope speculated that Gayoso's destination was Walnut Hills at the junction of the Yazoo and Mississippi rivers, and he then editorialized in his journal concerning the desire of James O'Fallon of the Yazoo Company to cultivate that region. He added, however, that the recently married O'Fallon, "having pitched his Tent in the Grotto of Miss *Clarke*, his Ardency, like his Constitution, will turn into downright Frigidity."[12]

Arriving in Natchez on March 27, Pope dallied there a week and recorded some of his most careful observations of his journey. He dined with Carlos de Grand-Pré, the commandant of the Spanish troops at the frontier outpost. Taking his leave of Grand-Pré and the citizens of Natchez, Pope continued down river with little to occupy his time except for casual observations about Loftus' Bluffs and Point Coupée and complaints about the "Musquettoes" which "harrassed" his party.

Pope was greatly intrigued by New Orleans. Landing there on April 4, he remained nearly six weeks, observing the physical aspects of the city, viewing its religious ceremonies, and judging its inhabitants' moral behavior by the standards of Alexander Pope. From New Orleans John Pope traveled to Pensacola—"the Metropolis of *West Florida*." After briefly describing the town, he reported that Governor Arturo O'Neill had informed him that in the eleven years he had lived in Pensacola "he had never experienced a Moments Sickness; and that all the Citizens enjoyed uninterrupted Health." Certainly such a boast—for whatever reason it may have been made—does not square with the facts. Pensacola had in the past and would continue to have problems with sickness, particularly those diseases endemic to the Gulf Coast, such as yellow fever. Pope does concede that illness was present among one class of residents, the Spanish soldier, "whose Mode of Living, will, at all Times, and in all Places, be productive of complicated Diseases. Inordinate Use of Ardent Spirits and bad Wine, superadded to high seasoned Meats and promiscuous Intercourse with lewd Women, will disorder any the most robust Habit of Body."

Pope also reported on the activities of the important Indian trading firm, Panton, Leslie and Company, that had its offices in Pensacola. His information concerning Panton's ownership of a salt works on New Providence Island and the general markup of 500 percent is basically accurate. In confirming these figures, William S.

Coker, editor and project director of "The Papers of Panton, Leslie and Co.," writes: "In general I would have to agree with Pope's comments. . . . We know there was a substantial mark up in the prices, but all justified on the grounds of the added cost to the company for getting it to the Indians via traders, etc. and, of course, on the problem involved in getting the skins to London. The risk of skins 'spoiling' or being ruined by worm damage was great, prices on the European market varied greatly, and insurance, shipping charges, etc. all brought the price of merchandise up considerably. So, 500% may not have been an unreasonable increase in prices."[13]

Pope departed Pensacola after a week, and together with an escort of eleven Indians, he entered Indian territory to visit Alexander McGillivray. Traveling as an "English Ambassador Incog."—a title which he labeled "ludicrous"—Pope arrived at McGillivray's house on the Coosa River on June 1, 1791, only to find that McGillivray was at his "upper Plantation," six miles farther up the river. It is here that the most intriguing part of Pope's trip unfolds. While visiting the Creek chief, whose father had been a Scotsman, Pope engaged in his usual observations and wrote among other things an account of the Indian ball games. Impressed with McGillivray's abilities, he included in his book two samples of the chief's writing in the form of hastily written letters which Pope was to deliver when he arrived back in Richmond.

The most interesting and intriguing part of Pope's visit with McGillivray, however, does not appear in Pope's published account of his tour. While at McGillivray's house Pope wrote a letter on June 4 to Tairux Wilcox of New Orleans in which he reported on his stay in Pensacola and his visit with the chief. In this letter, which is almost meaningless to the historian because of Pope's careful concealment of its intent, he concluded: "Ambiguity of expression must satisfy you now; as prudence forbids a full eclairecissement of *what* you are so anxious to know, see and enjoy."[14] By some unknown circumstance, McGillivray obtained a copy of Pope's letter, and on June 8, he wrote Estevan Miró concerning the Virginian's visit and letter to Wilcox. McGillivray reported that he was informed that Pope had "sketches and designs" of the forts at Natchez, New Orleans, and Pensacola and that Pope had been sent on his trip by "Enrique Clark of Kentucky" to obtain that information. He further added that Clark had been authorized by the state of Virginia to attack Spanish posts on the Mississippi and was preparing for such an adventure before the following spring. Undoubtedly McGillivray was referring to George Rogers Clark, for he mentioned that

Pope, who had recently visited Clark, had stated that Clark wanted the Indians to remain neutral "in case there should be a sudden attempt against the Spanish posts."[15]

While McGillivray reported that such an attack had been rumored for so long "that I did nothing other than laugh,"[16] clearly he felt the Spanish officials would wish to receive such intelligence. His expectations were correct, for on July 6, 1791, Miró informed McGillivray: "I received the information you gave me upon the famous Pope and will make proper use of it."[17] Eleven days later, Miró sent all of the correspondence to Luis de las Casas in Havana with his evaluation: "It [the letter from Pope to Wilcox] is very confused but I understand that it refers to the projected expedition of O'Fallon which Clark should be leading as he is his father-in-law."[18] Las Casas replied to Miró that as Pope had revealed the American plans, he was not a "true commissioner" but was a "despicable adventurer." Should Pope be a Spanish subject in Louisiana, las Casas ordered Miró to question him carefully concerning the American plans. If, however, Pope was not a Spanish subject, Miró was to reprimand the commanders at Natchez, New Orleans, and Pensacola for carelessly allowing a stranger to draw sketches of the posts.[19] Unfortunately, there is nothing to prove or discount the reports of espionage, and it must remain merely an intriguing episode in an otherwise mundane trip.

While among the Indians, Pope recorded much concerning their lives. Included is an Indian folk tradition concerning the Giant-King called Billy Pig whose foot could dam the Chattahoochee River; a description of their annual corn festival; a discussion of their methods of punishment for adultery, their burial ceremonies, and agricultural methods; and an extraordinary speech by an old "Conjuror" during a period of distress. Pope also included in his published account a list of Indian words and their translations.

Finally departing the Creek Nation in late June, Pope spent the next several weeks wandering through Georgia.[20] Crossing the Flint, Ocmulgee, and Oconee rivers, and passing through Washington (which he misplaced south of the Ogeechee River), he arrived at Augusta. Pope was pleasantly surprised by the village and predicted its future greatness. He also briefly visited with Georgia Governor Edward Telfair (whom he misnamed William). Proceeding down the Savannah River, Pope stopped briefly at Ebenezer and passed the "small and almost depopulated Town" of Purisburg before arriving at Savannah. He remained there only three days—mainly visiting Colonel Joseph Habersham and General Lachlan McIntosh—before he took passage on the schooner *Thomas*, which was bound for

Charleston. On board Pope found himself in the company of Senator Pierce Butler. Although the voyage was brief and quite rough, Pope described the senator as "a lively conversable Gentleman, possessed of a great Fund of Wit, sound Judgment, and good Breeding."[21]

Upon his arrival in Charleston on August 1, Pope took a room in M'Crady's Hotel (the same hotel in which George Washington stayed during his visit to Charleston earlier in 1791). Pope found the city's citizens to be "a gay, luxurious People, fond of Dress and pompous Equipage" and the city itself "eclipses all other Cities in the Union and is inferior to only Three in Size, Wealth, Population, Trade and Elegance of Buildings." While in Charleston, Pope visited the local dignitaries, including Colonel William Washington, and managed to mediate successfully a dispute which threatened to end in a duel.

Colonel Pope took the schooner *Exchange* from Charleston for his last bit of adventure before returning to the more settled regions of the United States. His destination was St. Marys, Georgia, on the river by the same name, but through an error the vessel entered the St. Johns River where the Spanish officials politely but firmly refused permission to land. Finally arriving at St. Marys, Pope found himself with little to do. He and a companion set out to explore the interior of East Florida. As they approached the "Neighbourhood of *St. Augustine*," they received repeated warnings to return to St. Marys. Although Pope admitted lacking prudence, the crew of his "small keel-bottomed Boat" made the decision for him and returned him and his companion to Georgia.

At this point in his narrative, Pope interrupted the flow of his account to present a five-page catalog of "medicinal Plants, Herbs, &c." which he "promised" some unknown being. Finally on September 2, Pope left St. Marys on the *Exchange* and arrived in New York thirteen days later after an uneventful trip.[22] He remained in New York for two weeks before journeying on by ship to Brunswick, New Jersey, and from there by stage through Princeton and Trenton on his way to Philadelphia. While it is not certain when Pope arrived there, it is clear that he was in Philadelphia on October 5, for on that date he met with Secretary of War Henry Knox and reported on his trip. It is evident from the memorandum that Knox wrote to himself concerning the visit that he had never met Colonel Pope, whom he described as "a man of candor and observation."[23] Pope apparently was equally impressed with Knox for, other than a sixteen-line apology for the type of book he had written, he closed it with "a few Lines of doggrel Verse," dedicated to and concerning Knox, Attorney General Edmund Randolph, and Philadelphia merchant Samuel Pleasants.

Although the book does not say so, presumably Pope returned to Richmond to write his account of his journey. It was a little over a year before the volume was ready to be offered to the public. John Dixon, who had recently moved from Williamsburg and who was editor of the *Virginia Gazette and Public Advertiser*, printed the book for Pope and his three children: Alexander D. Pope, Lucinda C. Pope, and Anne Pope. The first notice of its publication, however, appeared in James Carey's *Virginia Gazette & Richmond Daily Advertiser* on November 27, 1792: "The public are hereby notified, that COLOᴸ POPE'S JOURNAL is ready for delivery to the respective subscribers of this city and its vicinity. Those who reside at a remote distance may expect that care in deliverance, and dispatch in conveyance will be particularly attended to by Mr. John Dixon, printer, Richmond." The ad was repeated on December 7. It was not until December 29 that Dixon got around to printing an advertisement in his own paper, a notice which he repeated on January 12 and 19, 1793.[24] There is nothing in the advertisements to indicate the number of copies of the *Tour* that were printed or what they cost, but certainly Dixon and Pope would both be astounded to find a recent book dealer of "Southern Americana" offering the scarce 1792 edition for the sum of $14,000.[25]

One indication of the continuing interest in Pope's travel account is the history of its reprinting. While the mere republication of a work is certainly no valid measure of its worth, the work must be of sufficient interest to command the expense involved. The first reprint of Pope's *Tour* appeared in 1888. Charles L. Woodward, an obscure book dealer variously self-described as a "Book Peddler" and as a "dealer in Rare Books and Pamphlets Relating to America," announced his intention to publish a new printing of the book.[26] He announced that he would furnish copies for two dollars to those who ordered them in advance in order to defray the cost of his own copy. He asserted that there would be none printed beyond those ordered: "probably some few people who will not hear of it until it is too late to secure one will want to buy a copy, but they must not expect to buy mine."[27] Whether or not Woodward printed only those ordered and how many copies he printed is not known, but in 1888 the "Book Peddler" did reprint the 1792 edition with the addition of an index. The only other reprint edition of Pope's account was a 1971 reprint of the 1792 edition with no editorial additions.

Colonel John Pope's claim on the title page that the book will be of interest to everyone is obviously an overstatement. That it is a book of merit worth the attention of serious scholars of the late-eighteenth-century South is apparent. Pope's evaluation of the settlements he visited, of individuals with whom he talked, of the Indian tribes he observed, are all a part of the American tradition of personal travel accounts that must be consulted when trying to obtain an "accurate" picture of a subjective topic—the culture and society of the antebellum South. Pope's book has left its mark on America's heritage; unfortunately, the same cannot be said for the author, who vanished more rapidly than he appeared on the pages of American history.

ACKNOWLEDGMENTS.

While acknowledgments in a book of this nature may be unusual, because of the number of institutions that have attempted to help me track down the elusive Pope, I feel it incumbent upon me to express my gratitude to those depositories I visited. I am deeply indebted to the following institutions for their assistance and patience in opening their holdings to me: the Archives Division of the Virginia State Library, the Virginia Historical Society, the Historical Society of Pennsylvania, the National Archives (Atlanta branch), the Georgia Historical Society, the South Carolina Historical Society, the Charleston Library Society, the South Caroliniana Library of the University of South Carolina, the Southern Collection of the University of North Carolina at Chapel Hill, and the libraries of Louisiana State University, University of West Florida, Troy State University, Florida State University, University of Georgia, and Duke University. To the thirty-five or forty other institutions and individuals with whom I corresponded concerning Pope, I also wish to express my deepest appreciation.

The Troy State University Research Committee also provided funds which helped to defray the expenses involved in searching for Colonel John Pope.

University Presses of Florida wishes to express its appreciation to the Tracy W. McGregor Library of the University of Virginia for its assistance in the publication of this volume.

NOTES.

1. John Pope, *A Tour through the Southern and Western Territories of the United States of North-America* ... (Richmond, 1792), p. 19.

2. Thomas D. Clark, ed., *Travels in the Old South: A Bibliography* (Norman, 1956), 2:53; Samuel Cole Williams, ed., *Early Travels in the Tennessee Country, 1540–1800* (Johnson City, 1928), p. 317; Letter from John Melville Jennings, Director, Virginia Historical Society, December 21, 1976.

3. See John H. Gwathmey, *Historical Register of Virginians in the Revolution* (Richmond, 1938), p. 632; Louis A. Burgess, comp. and ed., *Virginia Soldiers in 1776* (Richmond, 1927), pp. 383–84.

4. Lenora Higginbotham Sweeny, *Amherst County, Virginia in the Revolution* (Lynchburg, 1951), pp. 35, 37, 38, 89, 97, 107, 127–28, 129, 131–33, 148, 154, 156, 163–64, 170.

5. *Heads of Families at the First Census of the United States Taken in the Year 1790: Records of the State Enumerations: 1782–1785: Virginia* (Baltimore, 1966), pp. 47, 84.

6. Amherst County Order Book, 1782–1784, Archives Division, Virginia State Library.

7. Amherst County Personal Property Books, 1782–1789, and Amherst County Land Tax Books, 1781–1792, Ar-

chives Division, Virginia State Library. It is not clear why Pope is listed in the latter source as the owner of the land for tax purposes while the same book shows the sale to Duval.

8. Richmond County Land Tax Books, 1785–1810, and Richmond County Personal Property Books, 1785–1812, Archives Division, Virginia State Library.

9. Memorandum, Oct. 5, 1791, Henry Knox Papers, 28:137. Microfilm, The Florida State University (hereafter cited as Knox Papers).

10. Samuel Guyton McLendon, *History of the Public Domain of Georgia* (Atlanta, 1924), pp. 35–36; Robert Douthat Meade, *Patrick Henry: Practical Revolutionary* (Philadelphia, 1969), pp. 422–23; William Wirt Henry, *Patrick Henry; Life, Correspondence and Speeches* (New York, 1891), pp. 507–8, 511–12. The Virginia Yazoo Company never received the land granted to it by the Georgia legislature. Despite Henry's charges of "Deception" and years of efforts, the company never obtained compensation for its efforts.

11. Pope, *Tour*, pp. 14–17. The *Pennsylvania Mercury* for September 4, 1790, reports on Brackenridge's marriage:

—Married—

Hugh H. Brackenridge, Esq. to Miss Sabina Wolf, a young girl of obscure German parents, on the waters of the Ohio; and has brought her to this city [Philadelphia] to spend the ensuing winter, and receive the advantage of some education.

'Tis easy to admire the flower
With which the gard'ner decked his bow'r;
Because, it must be excellent or rare,
Before his judgement could have plac'd it there:
But not so easy, in a wood or vale,
The virtues of a plant or flower to tell—
Discern its proper class—pronounce its name—
Select it thence, without least fear or blame,
And say it has a right to better place and fame.

See also Hugh Henry Brackenridge, *Modern Chivalry*, ed. Lewis Leary (New Haven, 1965), pp. 12–13; Daniel Marder, *Hugh Henry Brackenridge* (New York, 1967), pp. 48–49.

12. "Miss Clarke" is Francis Eleanor Clark, the sister of George Rogers Clark. Describing Miss Clark, O'Fallon writes: "I seen her by accident—, and married her in a fortnight afterwards. Veni, vidi, et vici: I am very happy. The Girl is young, amiable, and beautiful": O'Fallon to Henry Osborne, May 22, 1791, James O'Fallon Papers, 1791, Georgia Historical Society. For a biography of Gayoso, see Jack D. L. Holmes, *Gayoso: The Life of a Spanish Governor in the Mississippi Valley, 1789–1799* (Gloucester, 1968).

13. Letter from William S. Coker, July 26, 1977.

14. J. Pope to Tairux Wilcox, June 4, 1791, AGI, PC, leg. 2371; a Spanish translation is in AGS, leg. 6928. A copy of this letter is also in Lawrence Kinnaird, ed., *Spain in the Mississippi Valley, 1765–1794* (Washington, 1949), 3:411–12.

15. McGillivray to Miró, June 8, 1791, AGS, leg. 6928.

16. Ibid.

17. Miró to McGillivray, July 6, 1791, ibid.

18. Miró to las Casas, July 17, 1791, ibid.

19. Las Casas to Miró, Aug. 12, 1791, ibid. Copies of all this correspondence concerning the alleged espionage are also located in AGI, SD, leg. 2556 (microfilm copies located at Loyola University, New Orleans).

20. Pope later reported to Henry Knox that he stayed with McGillivray seven days and in the Creek Nation seven weeks. Memorandum, Oct. 5, 1791, Knox Papers, 28:137.

21. The sailing and arrival of the *Thomas*, with "Ross" as captain, is confirmed by the *Georgia Gazette* (Savannah), Aug. 4, 1791, and the *City Gazette* (Charleston), Aug. 2, 1791.

22. While Pope does not mention the specific date of his departure from St. Marys, the date of his arrival in New York, or the ship on which he was traveling, it is safe to assume that he was still aboard the *Exchange* with "Baine" as captain. He mentioned that he arrived after thirteen days' passage, and on September 15, 1791, the *Exchange* schooner arrived in New York from Charleston with "Bean" as captain. *The Federal Gazette and Philadelphia Daily Advertiser*, Sept. 16, 1791; *Pennsylvania Mercury, and General Advertiser* (Philadelphia), Sept. 20, 1791.

23. Memorandum, Oct. 5, 1791, Knox Papers, 28:137.

24. On Feb. 9, 1793, Dixon ran a notice in his paper that "On or before 10th day of March will be submitted to the inspection of the Public, A POEM entitled the DECEMVIRI, by John Pope." I have, however, been unable to locate a copy of this poem—if it was ever printed. *Virginia Gazette and Public Advertiser*, Feb. 9, 16, 1793.

25. Flier from Broadfoot's Bookmark, Wendell, N.C., June 1977.

26. Letter from The New York Public Library, Manuscripts and Archives Division, March 29, 1977.

27. Advertisement in *Catalogues Issued by Chas. L. Woodward; no. 1–45, 1876–1896;* original in New York Public Library.

A TOUR

THROUGH THE

SOUTHERN AND WESTERN TERRITORIES

OF THE

UNITED STATES

OF

NORTH-AMERICA;

THE

SPANISH DOMINIONS

ON THE RIVER MISSISSIPPI,

AND THE

FLORIDAS;

THE COUNTRIES OF THE

CREEK NATIONS;

AND MANY

UNINHABITED PARTS.

By JOHN POPE.

MULTORUM, PAUCORUM, PLURIUM, OMNIUM, INTEREST.

RICHMOND: PRINTED BY JOHN DIXON.

FOR THE AUTHOR AND HIS THREE CHILDREN, ALEXANDER D. POPE, LUCINDA C. POPE, AND ANNE POPE.

M,DCC,XCII.

TO THE
PUBLIC.

EVERY Man who commits his Sentiments to public Criticism, whether his Motive be Honor, Interest, or other Consideration, will be supposed to hope for Public Patronage, or Applause. But the Man who shall servily condefsend to obtain Success; who shall by debasing himself, attempt to elevate or exalt another, deferves not private Regard or Public Favor.

The Author of the following Sheets, is strongly impreffed with thefe Sentiments, and altho' he feels as all Authors must do, who commit themselves

to

to the World: Altho' he knows many great and respectable Men, whose Friendship would please him, and whose Patronage would do him Honor; he prefers to obtain their Assentation to his Labors, as the voluntary Effusions of their own Hearts, than as the Tribute to his Flattery or Solicitation. Thus thinking, none will blame, thus acting, all will applaud, who are admirers of the native Independancy, which is the Birth-right of Man.——

Inaccuracies will, in this Work, probably obtain, but let the Reader reflect, that it is the genuine Offspring of positive Observation, taken sometimes on Horseback, sometimes on a Stump, but always in Haste, amidst the Hurly Burly *of uninformed and generally Indian Companions.*

A TOUR,

A

T O U R, *&c.*

O N the firſt Day of *June*, 1790, I took my Departure from the City of *Richmond*, with an Intention of viſiting the Weſtern Regions of *Kentuckey*, and exploring the *Spaniſh* Dominions of *Louiſiana* and the two *Floridas*; as alſo the Territories of the *Creek* Nation, now under the Governance of *Alexander M'Gillivray*, Eſq; who from the concurrent Approbation which he hath merited and received from the whole Nation, may, with Propriety, be ſaid to hold imperial Power, having many Kings and Princes ſubordinate to him.

How far I have ſucceeded in the Exploration of thoſe Countries, the Reader will determine from a candid Peruſal of my Journal.

June 10th. Contracted a violent Rheumatiſm from wetting my Feet, in an Attempt to croſs the *Rapedan*, which retarded my Pro-

A 3

greſs

grefs for about eight Weeks in the County of *Culpeper*; where the Humanity and Politenefs of Col. *John Thornton* and his Lady mitigated my Diftrefs, and ultimately reftored me to my priftine Health and Vigour. This Gentleman, as well as his Brother *William*, poffeffes a rare mechanical Genius, and to which he hath fuperadded a practical Knowledge in Medicine and Surgery; the Advantages of which, his poor Neighbours often experience with Tears of Gratitude.

Some Years fince, the Affembly of Virginia voted a Premium to Mr. *John Hobdy*, for his Invention of a Machine, which he fubmitted to their Infpection, well calculated for the Purpofes of beating out Wheat and other fmall Grain. Col. *William* hath improved upon *Hobdy*'s Invention by conftructing a Water-Mill, which without the Aid of animal Exertion, fhatters out and prepares more fmall Grain of any Kind in one Day, than *Hobdy*'s can in one Week. With this Mill alone, he fpeedily prepares his Flax and Hemp for Market or the Diftaff. It is a Model well worth the Attention of every opulent Farmer, or of thofe who raife large Crops of Flax and Hemp.

Auguft

August 10. Croſſed the *Blue-Ridge*, and halted for three Days at *New-Town*, within about eight Miles of *Wincheſter*. This flouriſhing little Town I think, bids fair to eclipſe *Wincheſter* in a few Years, or, be connected with her by a lengthy Village: Its Locality gives it a decided Preference to *Wincheſter*, as being in a fertile Neighborhood, and nearer to Mills, Iron-Works and the future Navigation of the *Shenandoah*.

From this Place I made ſome few Excurſions into the Country, particularly to the Houſes of Colonels *Zane* and *Thruſton*; the former of whom poſſeſſes a greater Originality of Thought, Speech and Action, than any other Gentleman I ever was acquainted with.

> *O'er many Waters he hath been,*
> *And Knowledge great acquir'd,*
> *From reading Books as well as Men,*
> *For ſhining Parts admir'd:*
> *From ev'ry great Metropolis,*
> *He ſome Inſtruction draws,*
> *By aſcertaining its Police*
> *Of Manners, Cuſtoms, Laws.*

He is the Proprietor of the Iron-Works, which, under his judicious Management yield an amazing Profit. All the Works which are very complex, are driven by the Water iſ-

A 4

ſuing

fuing from one Spring, whofe Source is not above a Quarter of a Mile from the Spot.

Auguft 14th. Found myfelf happy in the Family of the fenfible, humane and generous Col. *G. M. Thrufton*, whofe public and private Characters will bear the ftricteft Scrutiny. His late Difplay of unparralled Generofity to a diftreffed, though reputable Family, will be enrolled in the Court above; and from the recording Angel, inftead of a Tear, extort an approbative Smile. This Gentleman at an early Period of the War, laying afide his facerdotal Habit, appeared at the Head of a Regiment in Defence of his injured Country. His Achievements in the Field, his Wifdom in Council, and the general Tenour of his Conduct, through the various Scenes of Life, do him Honour, and claim from a grateful Country its warmeft Acknowledgments.

On this Gentleman's Farm I obferved about an Acre of Ground well befet with *Jerufalem* Artichokes, of a most luxuriant Growth ; the Colonel told me that he was confident the Production would exceed one Thoufand Bufhels. To this Vegetable, Swine and horned Cattle of every Defcription, particularly Sheep, are furprifingly attached—I do not difcover it to

be

be any Way inferiour to the Garden Artichoke for Table Ufe.

Auguſt 17th.   Arrived in *Wincheſter* much relaxed from the Heat of the Weather, and whilſt lolling on a Couch, was faluted by a Mr. *John Welch*, who had ferved in my Regiment in the Capacity of a common Soldier during the laſt War.   With great Self-Complacency he informed me, that ſince the War he had been profperous in Life, had acquired a fnug little Retreat in the Country, and then had a large Drove of Cattle within four Miles of the Place, which he meant to difpofe of to the *French* emigrants then ſtationary in *Wincheſter*—that he wiſhed to go back, meet the Drove and hurry them into Town, leaſt others might fupplant him in the Sale; but that he had fent his Horfe to the fame Paſture where his Cattle were, fo that he ſhould be under the Neceſſity of going on Foot, unlefs he could beg, borrow or ſteal a Nag to ride that fmall Diſtance: Mr. *Welch*, I am happy to hear of your Profperity, and you are entirely welcome to the Ufe of my Horfe to ride that Diſtance— Sir, you are very good, and I'll embrace your generous Offer, and on my Return this Evening give myfelf the Pleafure of Dining with you.   I fear fome Accident has happened to Mr. *Welch*, as I have neither feen him, the

Horfe

Horſe, Bridle or Saddle from that Hour to this! In this Situation, on a Journey with 180 Miles in Rear, and 500 in Front, I began like *Strap* to moralize, with only this Difference, he ſaid "A Fool and his Money is ſoon parted;" I uſed the Word Horſe inſtead of Money.

During my Continuance in *Wincheſter*, I was frequently in the Company of General *Morgan*, whoſe Character as a Military Man, is held in high Eſtimation even by his Enemies—Poſſeſſed of an eaſy Fortune, he now enjoys all the Sweets of Domeſtication, and the Heart felt Pleaſure ariſing from a conſcious Rectitude. He is fond of the ſocial Pleaſures, and will ſometimes in his gayer Moments, amuſe the Company with Narratives of martial Feats, and how Somebody, and who it was, that plucked the Laurels from fierce Tarlton's Brow.

September. Hearing that the *Monongalia* and *Ohio* were innavigable, I reſolved to ſpend my Time until they ſhould riſe among my Friends in *Berkeley* County, which for its Temperature of Air, Salubrity of Baths and Fertility of Soil, juſtly claims the Preference of every other County in *Virginia*, but leſs ſo of *Frederick* than the reſt, whether for the
Properties

Properties already mentioned, or the Hofpitality and Independence of its People in general.

I paid a Vifit to Mr. *Charles Wafhington*, the Brother of our beloved Prefident, where I had the Pleafure of feeing a moft affectionate Meeting between him and his Sifter, attended with feveral Female Relations from *Frederickfburg*. Mr. *Robert Rutherford*, a Member of the *Virginia* Senate was alfo there, and contributed much to the Chearfulnefs of the Company, by finging feveral moft excellent and fentimental Songs. I am indebted to this Gentleman and Mr. *Wafhington* for furnifhing me with a joint Letter of Introduction, to fome of the moft reputable Characters in *Kentuckey*: Meffrs. *David Gray* and *Mofes Hunter* are among the number of thofe who have impofed Obligations on me.

October. Purfued my Route through *Shepherd*'s Town and *Martinfburg*, two flourifhing little Towns. At the former I faw General *Gates* and his Family on their Way to *New-York*, and at the latter, General *Stephen*, who obferved that the Triumvirate was now entirely diffolved, alluding to Generals *Lee, Gates* and himfelf:

Whom

Whom Dame Fortune in a merry Mood,
Concenter'd in one Neighbourhood ;
Evincing well, that Birds of Feather,
Always chirp and flock together.

Began to afcend the *Alleghany* Mountains in Company with old Col. *Shepherd*, who obferved that for many Years he had made it an invariable Rule to take a hearty Drink of Grog at a Spring near the Road-Side, where the Eaftern and Weftern Waters very amicably take their Leave of each other, intimating that we and our Weftern Brethren ought to do fo likewife. I fhall not undertake a Defcription of a Sixty Miles Paffage over thofe *Alpine* Hills, but content myfelf with faying, that I paffed through the Shadow of Death—faw General *Wafhington*'s Intrenchment at the Meadows, and undifmayed, rode over *Braddock*'s Grave. From the Weftern Side of *Laurel* Hill, on a pleafant Evening, I was ravifh'd with the Profpect of Beefon Town and the circumjacent Country. Ten Miles from Beefon Town lies the Old Fort, at the Junction of a fmall Stream, called *Redftone*, and the *Monongalia*. At this Place we were detained about a Week, experiencing every Difguft which Rooks and Harpies could excite.

October.

October.   Went on Board a *Kentuckey* Boat in Company with three *Danville* Merchants, and a Mr. *Fooley* from the State of *Maryland*, and in Twenty-three Hours reached *Pittsburg.* The laſt mentioned Gentleman from his Singularities and Fooleries merits a minute Deſcription, which, however, I am at a Loſs to give. Suffice it to ſay, that Mr. *Thomas Fooley*, of a very reputable Family in *Maryland*, is about ſix Feet three Inches high, and every Way diſproportionate in his Shape and contradictory in the Lineaments of his Face, which at firſt View excited a Reſibility in the moſt ſerious Beholder. The Deformities of his Conduct vie with thoſe of his Perſon. It was ſometime laſt Month that Mr. *Fooley* eloped from his Lady, under an Apprehenſion that ſhe was preparing through the Medium of her Friends an Inſtrument of Writing for him to ſign, whereby a conſiderable Part of his Fortune was to be veſted in the Hands of Truſtees, ſubject to her Controul. To this Mr. *Fooley* was utterly oppoſed—However, previous to his Elopement he left her an unlimited Power of Attorney, which he delivered into the Hands of his Overſeer. At *Redſtone* he diſpoſed of his elegant Horſe and Furniture for an old Braſs Watch, which has the Property of being

right

right once in every Twelve Hours: Notwithstanding this, Mr. *Fooley* is a Gentleman of Refinement, being both a Philosopher and Politician, with some Knowledge of Astrology and Palmistry.

October.   Apprehending a Return of the Rheumatism, I resolved to awart the Event in *Pittsburg*, where I could be comfortably lodged and duly attended; I staid ten Days. Here I saw the celebrated *Hugh Henry Breckenridge*, Author of the six political Sermons in the beginning of the War, and of various other Traits since—He had been lately married to a Miss *Sabina Wolfe*, Daughter of an old *Dutch* Farmer in *Washington* County— The Circumstances of his Courtship, Marriage and subsequent Conduct I shall relate, with some slight References to the Person, Temper and Disposition of the Man.

Mr. *Breckenridge* on his Way from *Washington* Court, called in at Mr. *Wolfe*'s to have his Horse fed and escape a Rain which was then descending. The Horse was fed, the Rain had subsided, and Mr. *Breckenridge* to avoid wet Feet, ordered his Horse to be brought to the Door; Miss *Wolfe* was directed to perform that Office.

Nut

Nut brown were her Locks, her Shape was full ftrait,
Her Eyes were as black as a Sloe ;
Milk white were her Teeth, full fmart was her Gait,
And fleek was her Skin as a Doe.

Thefe Allurements made a deep Impreffion upon the fufceptible Heart of *Breckenridge*—He prevented her in the fervile Office, mounted his Nag and off he went. He had not gone more than a Sabbath Day's Journey, (for fuch his really was) before his Horfe, at the Inftigation of the Rider, turned fhort about and revifited Mr. *Wolfe*'s. A familiar Application was made to the old Gentleman for his Daughter, which he confidered as nothing more than Pleafantry in Mr. *Breckenridge*, for which he is fo remarkable. Mr. *Breckenridge* declared that he was ferious, that his Intentions were honourable, and that this future Happinefs refted on the Event of his then Application. Mifs *Sabina* had been employed in Shrubbing the old Man's Meadow, which faved him the annual Expence of about ten Dollars. This with him was an infuperable Objection to parting with his Girl—Mr. *Breckenridge* obviated the Difficulty by paying down a Sum of Money, obtained the Young Lady's Confent, married her, and fent her to *Philadelphia*, where fhe now is under the Governance of a reputable

female

female Character, whofe Bufinefs will be to polifh the Manners, and wipe off the Rufti-cities which Mrs. *Breckenridge* had acquired whilft a *Wolfe*.

As an Introduction to an Acquaintance with this Gentleman, I compofed, inclofed and fent to him on the Evening of my Arri-val, the following hafty Production, which without my Knowledge or Confent, he had inferted in the *Pittfburg* Gazette.

To H. H. Breckenridge, *Efq*; *on his being fairly* noos'd.

THY great and independent Soul did tow'r,
And from the faireft Stalk felect the Flow'r:
Which in the Wild unknown to public View,
In mild Pudicity fo fweetly grew.
Sabina learn! It was not giddy Chance,
That led fair Merit up to high Advance?
No, 'twas Heaven which open'd on his Eyes,
When Love and he firft view'd thee with Surprize.
The Matron fhall e'er long by him be taught,
To fpeak and act aboon the vulgar Thought.
His plaftic Hand fhall fafhion and fo mould,
And turn as 'twere, thy unwrought Ore to Gold.
That neither in Idea nor Romance,
Or in Metropolis of polifh'd France;
Shall any Dame be found to equal thee,
In Manners foft, and true Gentility.

Thus

Thus augur I of thee, oh purele∫s Dame,
Whose Conduct ∫oon ∫hall ∫well the Trump of Fame.
And well evinc'd when form'd on Wi∫dom's Plan,
Who can reward and ∫oothe an hone∫t Man.

In Company with this Gentleman I viewed the Fort and neighbouring Eminencies of *Pitt∫burg*, which will one Day or other employ the hi∫toric Pen, as being replete with ∫trange and melancholy Events. The Town at pre∫ent, is inhabited with only ∫ome few Exceptions, by Mortals who act as if po∫∫e∫∫ed of a Charter of Exclu∫ive Privilege to filch from, annoy and harra∫s her Fellow Creatures, particularly the incautious and nece∫∫itous; many who have emigrated from various Parts to *Kentuckey* can verify this Charge—Goods of every De∫cription are dearer in *Pitt∫burg* than in *Kentuckey*, which I attribute to a Combination of pen∫ioned Scoundrels who infe∫t the Place.

" Some Men in Pow'r and Tru∫ts, have made
" The one Hand with the other trade ;
" Gain'd va∫tly by their joint Endeavour,
" The right a Thief, the left Receiver ;
" And what the one by Tricks fore∫tall'd,
" The other by as ∫ly retail'd."

HUDIBRAS.

B Was

Was a *Spaniard* to reside among the *Pittf-burgers* only one Week, he would be apt to exclaim in the Words of *Quevedo*:

> " *Menca la cola el Can,*
> " *No por ti fino por el Pan.*"

TRANSLATED.

> ' *Tis not for thee ; but for thy Bread,*
> *Tray wags his Tail and fhakes his Head.*

November. I proceeded down the *Ohio* in Mr. *Beall*'s Boat, which was a moveable Fortification ; having about one Hundred and Fifty Salt Pans fo arranged, as to render a few Men within, capable of repulfing ten Times their Number without. Nothing materially occurred—We had a tolerable Paffage of five Days and Nights down to *Limeftone*, a little Town, fituate on the Banks of the *Ohio*, at the Mouth of *Limeftone* Creek, where Emigrants from *Virginia* and all the Eaftern States moft commonly debark. Leaving this Place, I paffed on in a direct Route through the moft fertile Parts of *Kentuckey*, by *Wafh-ington*, *Bourbon* and *Lexington* Townfhips to *Danville*, the prefent Metropolis of the Diftrict. In this Place and its Vicinage I continued about a Month, experiencing every Civility and Hofpitality which fo remarkably

charac-

characterize the People. The Topography of *Kentuckey* is foreign to my Purpose, as Mr. *Filfon* and others have treated that Subject with great Candour and Preciffion. Mere Occurrencies, and the moft confpicuous Traits of Men and Manners, are the principal Objects of my Inveftigation. General *Wilkinfon* and *Scott* are too generally known both at Home and abroad, to require any Eulogium from me : I fhall, therefore, wifhing them every Profperity, proceed on to *Louifville* and its Neighbourhood, and roufe up Gen. *George Rogers Clarke*, who, the *Kentuckians* fay, hath actually been in a profound Slumber for upwards of four Years, without the leaft Symptoms of Wakefulnefs whatever.

December 15th. Arrived at his Houfe under an Apprehenfion that he had forgotten me. He immediately recognized me, and without Ceremony, entered into a familiar, though defultory Converfation, in which I was highly pleafed with the Atticifm of his Wit, the genuine Offspring of native Genius. On ferious and important Occafions he difplays a Profundity of Judgment, aided by Reflection and matured by Experience. I cannot difmifs this Gentleman without obferving, that fome few Years fince he fhone forth in all the Glory of military Prowefs.

B 2

He

He appeared from his Plans and Succeſſes to have poſſeſſed an intuitive Knowledge of the Manœuvres and Deſigns of the Enemy, having in no Inſtance out of many concerted his Operations injudiciouſly.

At *Louiſville* the firſt Objeĉt that caught my Attention was the ludicrous Mr. *Fooley*—Having exhauſted all his Caſh, he had exchanged his fine long tail'd broad Cloth Coat for a Sailor's coarſe Jerkin, which reached within four Inches of the Waiſtband's of his red Pluſh Breeches—He had ſwapped his Beaver for a coarſe high crown'd narrow brimm'd Wool Hat, which he thought expedient, though contrary to all Precedent, to throw into a ſmart triangular Cock ; by the laſt Exchange he gained a round Half Dollar Piece. In this Garb, our Hero fraught with confummate Impudence, ſet out in Queſt of Adventures. As he had been a Fellow Traveller in a ſtrange Land, I could not help remonſtrating with him upon the Impropriety of his Conduĉt, which, however he endeavoured to defend, by obſerving that his then Appearance was in Honour to the Memories of Mr. *Sterne* and Lord *Verulam*.—For Sir, added he, Mr. *Sterne*, hath written expreſsly on the Subjeĉt of Jerkins in theſe Words, " A Man's Body and his Mind, with reverence I ſpeak
it,

it, are exactly like a Jerkin and a Jerkin's Lining—Rumple the one, you Rumple the other:" And as to my Lord *Verulam*, "*Smell-fungus* in his Hiſtory of *England* repreſents his Lordſhip's Chappo, as ſimilar to what now covers the Noddle of your humble Servant."

In the Neighbourhood of *Louiſville* I continued upwards of two Months; thoſe with whom I aſſociated, were affable and humane : The Stranger here may conſider himſelf as at Home—for ſuch is the extreme Hoſpitality of the People, that unknown to their Gueſt, they will confer, or rather impoſe Acts of Beneficence, which cannot be refuſed without Rudeneſs.

March 4th. 1791. Proceeded down the *Ohio* in Company with a *Frenchman*, who was taking his *American* Wife and Children along with him to *Langue la Graiſſe*, or, the *Greaſy Bent* ; now called by the *Spaniards Neuvo Madrid*, on the Weſtern Side of the *Miſſiſippi*. The Governor of *Penſacola* ſays, that the Etymology of *Langue la Graiſſe* originates from the Rivers forming an extenſive Curve; where, upon the firſt Settlement of the Place, great Quantities of Bear-Meat were ſtored up for the Uſe of the Garriſon and
the

the *French* and *Spanish* Navigators up and down the *Missisippi*, which Meat is of a very oleose Quality ; though in my Opinion, the Greasiness of the Soil, with the Devexity of the River, sufficiently justify the Epithet.

During our Passage from *Louisville* to this Place, we were frequently alarmed at the hostile Appearance of Indians on both Sides of the *Ohio* and *Missisippi* ; suspecting our Numbers to be superiour to their own, they were deterred from coming against us in Force ; which had they done, we should have fallen Victims without a Possibility of Escape to their merciless Barbarity.

March 12th. 1791. Breakfasted and dined with *Signior Pedro Foucher*, Commandant at *Neuvo Madrid*. The Garrison consist of about Ninety Men, who are well supplied with Food and Raiment ; they have an excellent Train of Artillery, which appears to be their chief Defence—Two Regular Companies of Musqueteers with charged Bayonets might take this Place. Of this Opinion is the Commandant himself, who complains that he is not sufficiently supported—He is a *Creole* of *French* Extraction, of *Patagonian* Size, polite in his Manners, and of a most noble Presence. On the Evening of this Day embarked

barked in a Boat called the Smoke-Houſe, bound to *New Orleans*, and anchored on the *Georgian* Shore, about Thirty Miles below *Madrid*.

13th. Setting at the Veſſel's Head I eſpied about a Dozen Fowls as large as *Muſcovite* Ducks, of a bluiſh grey Colour, with remarkable ſhort Necks, the Name of which no one on Board knew, as never having ſeen any of the Kind before, though they had long been accuſtomed to the Navigation of the *Miſſiſippi*, and viſited moſt Parts of the habitable Globe. An *Hibernian* on Board ſwore that from the ſhortneſs of their Necks they were either *Cygnets* or young *Cranes* ; for that the old Ones had Necks ten Times as long.

14th. The Trees on the Margin of the River in Verdue. At 9 o'Clock encounted a Congeries of Aiots and paſſed the firſt *Chickaſaw* Bluff, where the River is about Five Hundred Yards wide—At 12 o'Clock we loſt Sight of *Monſieur*'s Boat in a ſtrong Gale of Wind—8 o'Clock at Night one of Mr. *Craig*'s Tobacco Boats, with Forty Hogſheads of Tobacco, and a large Quantity of Flour and Plank paſſed us whilſt we lay in Harbour, ſhe had loſt her Rudder and ſprung a Leak

a Leak. In this Situation, with only three
Hands on Board, they implored our Aid,
which through prudential Motives was denied.

15th. At Sunrife efpied the *Frenchman*'s
Boat in good Harbour and uninjured; but
different was the Fate of Mr. *Craigs*, which
had fprung a Leak in her Bow and appeared
to be ftranded oppofite to the fecond *Chick-
afaw* Bluff, where the River is about Four
Hundred Yards wide. At 9 o'Clock we
viewed the third *Chickefaw* Bluff, oppofite
to the *Bayone St. John*, where the River is
not quite Four Hundred Yards wide. The
Colours of this Bluff are white, red, yellow,
blue, grey, black, brown, purple, &c. Here
the *Chickafaws* once had a fmall Pottery—
Upon this Bluff is the moft eligible Situation
for a Town which I have as yet feen on the
Banks of the *Miffifippi.*—Juft under this
Bluff, within fix Feet of the Shore, a firft
Rate Man of War might ride in Safety, un-
affailed by Winds, &c. At the upper End
of this Bluff is an old Blockhoufe, built by
a Captain *Befheare*'s Company, who had the
Convoy of military Stores for the *Chickafaws*,
which they depofited therein, until they
could procure the Affiftance of additional and
frefh Hands. From the lower End of this
Bluff,

Bluff, the River fuddenly opens to the amazing width of four, five and fixth Miles. Upon Examination, I find our Crew confift of one *Irifhman,* one *Anfpacher,* one *Kentuckean,* one Perfon born on *Sea,* one *Virginian,* and one *Welchman*; fix Total. At 12 o'Clock came on a violent Storm, which with Difficulty we evited, by exerting every Nerve to gain the Shore.

March 17th. 1791. The *Irifhman* in Honour of St. *Patrick,* purloined all our Brandy, Sugar and Eggs to make a Tub of Egg-Nog, of which he drank fo copioufly, that whilft at the Helm, he infenfibly run the Veffel into a ftrong Eddy, to get her out of which, employed all Hands in hard Labour the Balance of the Day.

March 18th. At Sunrife came on a flight Snow, which formed a curious Contraft to the Verdure of the Trees—All the Afternoon of this Day we run due North.

19th. At 8 o'Clock we run due South—All this Day the Weather was intenfely cold, the Wind blowing from North. About Noon fix *Indians* of the *Chaffaw* Nation came on Board and prefented us with two Strings of jerked Venifon, for which we in Return gave
C
them

them ſix Pound of Bacon and a Peck of Salt, which they pronounced to be very good. At 1 o'Clock we were hailed by a *Pennſylvanian* and a Lad in a *Peroch*, laden with Bear and Buffaloe Meat, taken on the St. *Francis* River, and bound up the *Oſarque* River, where there is a Settlement of Thirty Families about Thirty Miles from its Mouth. At 3 o'Clock overtaken by two Boats laden with Flour and Tobacco.

20th. At Sunriſe drew up a Kitten of about Twenty lbs. Weight, which with the Help of GOD and an *Iriſh* Cook, we made into moſt excellent Broth. At 9 o'Clock came up with two large *Pittſburg* Boats at Anchor laden with Flour, on the Shore, oppoſite to which, was a Concourſe of *Oſarque Indians*. An old Man among them was in Mourning, having his Face blacken'd over with a Commixture of Bear's Oil, Charcoal and Turpentine: Juſt under his Jowls were two Streaks of red and white, which ran parallel to each other—The *Indian* Ladies very innocently diſplayed their Navels, and the curious Eye might have explored other Parts which civilized Nations induſtriouſly conceal. Twenty Miles up the *Oſarque* River are their Wigwams, oppoſite to which, on the Eaſtern Side, is a *Spaniſh* Garriſon of Twenty-nine Men—
The

The Place is high, well watered, and as yet the Garrifon have experienced no Sicknefs.

21ft. At 8 o'Clock defcried a Keel bottom'd Boat with a fquare Sail, bound to *New Madrid*—Her Progrefs under a fair Wind was at the Rate of two and a half Miles per Hour, which might have been accelerated by the Addition of Oars. At ten o'Clock entered a narrow Part of the *Miffifippi*, where it is not more than Two Hundred Yards wide. At 12 o'Clock difcovered another Keel bottom'd Boat, deftined to the fame Place with the former. At Sunfet, three of Mr. *Craig*'s Tobacco Boats came up with us whilft we lay in Harbour, the fourth being ftill under the Command of the Rear Admiral, whofe Intrepidity hath often endangered his Veffel by oppofing the poor *Planters* and *Sawyers*, who have taken up their Refidence in this fpacious River. It is fhrewdly fufpected that the Rear Admiral will be tried by a Board of *Dons*, fo foon as he makes the Port of *Natchez*.

22d. At Sunrife, efpied a Veffel of General *Wilkinfon*'s, under the Command of Captain *Swaine*, bound to *New Orleans*—At 8 o'Clock we had in View fix Sail of the Line.

                    22d.

23d. At 12 o'Clock we ran North Weft-wardly—Here the *Miſſiſippi* forms on the *Spaniſh* Side an exact Reſemblance of an Horſe Shoe.

24th. At Break of Day eſpied the Walnut Hills about ten Miles below the *Yaſous* River, which his Catholic Majeſty limits as his Boundary, and below which, his Vice-gerents ſay, that Citizens of the *United States* ſhall not inhabit, unleſs they throw themſelves under the Laws, Banners and Protection of the King of *Spain*. At 10 o'Clock eſpied a Shingle roofed Houſe, occupied by a Family of *New-Yorkers*—Near this Spot the Governor of the *Natchez* hath fixed upon an Eminence for the Erection of a Fort. The Family informed, that the intended Garriſon were at the *Natchez*, taking in military Stores and Proviſion. The River oppoſite to the intended Fort is about Six hundred Yards wide. Whoever undertakes a Deſcription of the *Walnut* Hills, muſt have a fertile Imagination, be happy at Landſcape Painting, and uſe Something like Romance, or he will fall infinitely ſhort of that Eulogium which the Place ſo juſtly merits.

23d. At Sunriſe, ſaw two ſmall Houſes on the Eaſtern Side of the River upon a beautiful

tiful Eminence, from whence runs off a great Extent of very level fertile Ground : The Eminencies refemble the round Hills of *Stafford* County, in the *Northern Neck* of *Virginia.* At 2 o'Clock I went on Board the Governor of *Natchez'* Barge, his Name is *Gayofo.* Here I was regaled with delicious Nuts and excellent Wines. This Gentleman has a majeftic Deportment, foftened by Manners the moft engaging and polite. Having been brought up at the Court of *London,* he is well acquainted with the Etiquette of Mortals who move in the more exalted and fplendid Scenes of Life. He had in Company with him two Victualling Boats and an armed Schooner, laden with military Stores. I could not afcertain their Deftination, tho' it was probably to the *Walnut* Hills. His Soldiery including Mariners and Mechanics, did not exceed one Hundred Men. Doctor *O'Fallan,* Agent for the *Yafous* Company, ardently pants for the Cultivation of this delicious Soil ; but by Connoifeurs, it is fhrewdly conjectured, that having pitched his Tent in the Grotto of Mifs *Clarke,* his Ardency, like his Conftitution, will turn into downright Frigidity.

24th. At Sunrife, we fhot the Grand Gulph, oppofite to which, on either Side,
the

the Cane grows to the enormous Height of Forty and fometimes Forty-five Feet. At 8 o'Clock an impervious Fog arofe, fo as to prevent a Difcovery of *Sawyers* and other Obftacles not more than ten Feet from us. It might with Propriety have been called " Darknefs vifible." At 9 o'Clock paffed the *Bayone Pierre*, on the Banks of which are three fmall Houfes and about Thirty Acres of Ground under Cultivation—About ten Miles higher up the Country it is pretty thickly inhabited by *Virginians, Carolineans, Georgians*, and fome few Stragglers from the Eaftern States.

26th. At Sunrife came in Sight of the Town of *Natchez*, fituate on the Eaftern Bank of the River. It contains about an Hundred Houfes, and is the Metropolis of the Diftrict and Refidence of *Don Gayofo*, the Governor laft mentioned. In this Town and its Vicinage we continued about a Week.

27th. On *Sunday* I took a View of the Governor's Palace, as alfo of the Fort; which from its elevated Situation has a fine Command of the River for about a Mile up, and double that Diftance down it : though I think it might be affailed with Succefs by a

fingle

fingle Regiment, or taken by Surprize with a lefs Number. The lying of the back Ground, and the Paucity and Infignificance of the Garrifon would favour either Plan. They have a good Train of Artillery, though very injudicioufly arranged; the back Part of the Fort being *pregnable* to a Dozen Men.

28th. Paid a Vifit to *Don Granfrey*, Commandant of the Regular Forces throughout the *Natchez* Diftrict: he lives about Two Miles from Town. Here I was regaled with different Kinds of Fruits, Wines and Parmefan Cheefe, which were fucceedent to a very good fubftantial Dinner. Hofpitality and Urbanity prefided at his Board: His Lady is young, handfome and polite—His Vifitants confifted of five reputable Gentlemen and three Ladies. One of the Gentlemen fpoke the *Englifh* and *Spanifh* Languages with great Propriety and Eafe. Him we fixed upon as Linguift to the Company, and through whom we carried on a brifk and chearful Converfation. The *Spanifh* Gentlemen and Ladies with whom I had an Opportunity of converfing, do not poffefs that Aufterity and Referve, which are fo generally afcribed to their Nation. The Character of the *Spaniards* is thus drawn by the celebrated **Mr.**

Mr. *Swinburne*, after his late Travels through the Country.

"The *Catalans* appear to be the moſt active, ſtirring Set of Men, the beſt calculated for Buſineſs, Travelling and Manufactures—The *Valencians* a more ſullen, ſedate Race, better adapted to the Occupations of Huſbandry, leſs eager to change Place, and of a much more timid, ſuſpicious Caſt of Mind than the former—The *Andaluſians* ſeem to be the greateſt Talkers and Rhodomontadoes of *Spain*—The *Caſtilians* have a manly Frankneſs, and leſs Appearance of Cunning and Deceit—The *New Caſtilians* are perhaps the leaſt induſtrious of the whole Nation—The *Old Caſtilians* are laborious, and retain more of antient Simplicity of Manner ; both are of a firm determined Spirit—The *Arragoneſe* are a Mixture of the *Caſtilian* and *Catalan*, rather incling to the former—The *Biſcayners* are acute and diligent, fiery and impatient of Control, more reſembling a Colony of Republicans, than a Province of an abſolute Monarchy—And the *Galacians* are a plodding Painſtaking Race of Mortals, that roam over *Spain* in Search of an hardly earned Subſiſtence."

From this Deſcription ; thoſe with whom I converſed are certainly *Caſtilians*, or of that Pedigree.

Pedigree. To Mr. *Swinburne's* Character of the Nation I ſhall have frequent Reference, as I ſhall be much among them, and probably ſee Mortals anſwering each provincial Deſcription. About ſome ten or fifteen Miles above the Town of *Natchez*, lies the Settlement of the *Bayoue Pierre*—It comprehends a Neighbourhood of about Thirty Miles in Length and Twenty Miles in Width, compoſed generally of People who have moved, and ſtill continue to move in elevated Stations, when compared to thoſe, who, though now poſſeſſed of Wealth, uſhered into Life without the Advantages of Fortune, Family, or Education.

29th. At the *Natchez* I obſerved an Advertiſement relating to a ſtray Horſe, for the Setting up of which, the Owner was obliged to get the previous Sanction of a Magiſtrate. An Inhabitant under the Juriſdiction of *Spain* may be ſaid to be,

" *Homo ſine Spe, ſine Sede, ſine Re.* "

The Soil of this Diſtrict is better adapted to the Growing of Corn, Rice and Indigo, than of Tobacco, the Cultivation of which, is gradually falling into Diſuſe; as an Admittance of it into the King's Store is now

D   poſitively

positively refused, from some political Motives, which the Governor thinks himself under no Obligation to communicate; though the present Crop was raised under a Confidence reposed in his Promise, to receive and allow eight Dollars per Hundred for it.

30th. At 10 o'Clock discovered the Wreck of one of Mr. *Craig*'s Tobacco Boats, which he had directed to be got under Way. Into this Boat, exclusive of Tobacco, he had stowed a considerable Quantity of Bacon, Butter, Flour and Plank—He lost almost the whole. His Boatsmen (for whom he now no longer had Occasion) appeared to bear his Loss with great Composure and Christian Fortitude. At 1 o'Clock moved from the *Natchez*, and in two Hours viewed the white Bluff on the Eastern Side of the River. This Situation is Romantic and boasts a Gentleman's Seat, near which lay three large Tobacco Boats unlaunched. Mr. *Ellis*, from *Amelia* County, of *Virginia*, resides at this Place. Here I discovered the first Pine Trees since I crossed the *Allegheny* Mountains.

31st. At 12 o'Clock past *Loftus*'s Bluff, where the River is about Two Hundred Yards wide. This Situation is beauteous, and has two Plantations on the summit laid off in oblong

long Squares, and a little Way below, a fine extenfive Meadow. At 3 o'Clock hailed by a Row Galley from *New Orleans*, bound to *New Madrid*. At 4 o'Clock efpied the Long Reach, where the Eye may take in an uninterrupted Water Profpect of Twenty-three Miles. At our Entrance into the Long Reach we viewed the Red River, about a Quarter of a Mile wide, on the Weftern Side of the *Miffifippi*; and three Miles below it the *Bayoue Chappaliere*, which taking its Leave of this River, difembogues its gentle Stream into the Gulph of *Mexico*, feveral Leagues from the Mouths of the *Miffifippi*.

April 1ft. At Sunrife we heard the Reville beaten on the Weftern Side of the River, where there is a fmall *Spanifh* Garrifon.

2d. Hailed by two Perochs, one bound to the *Natchez*, the other to the *Bayoue Pierre*. For two Days paft we have been much harraffed by *Mufquettoes*—The poor *Indians* who go almoft naked, conftruct an elevated Bed of Reeds, which they Suffumigate, fo as to banifh Infects of every Defcription from their Lodgements. Slight whitewafhed airy Buildings become more common on the Eaftern Side of the River, and are, in general, occupied by People from the *United States*.

D 2 Here

Here are the moſt delightful Proſpects that ever caught my View—On the Weſtern Side there is a Meadow three Miles in Length and Half a Mile in Width, beſet with *Engliſh* Clover about eighteen Inches high, which depaſtures about Three Hundred Head of Horſes, and an equal Number of horned Cattle.

3d. At 10 o'Clock viewed *Point Coupee,* a Village Twenty-one Miles in Length, though narrow, conſiſting of inferiour Buildings, interſperſed now and then with dwelling Houſes, and Chapels of tolerable Elegance. At 4 o'Clock ſaw eight Country Seats on the Eaſtern Bank, and at the lower End of ſome high Bluffs, a large Building of extraordinary Workmanſhip, and a Dock-yard about Half a Mile below it. At 6 o'Clock viewed the *Alexandrian* Bluffs, from which on both Sides of the River there is a Continuation of beauteous Farms and elegant Buildings for the Diſtance of Sixty-one Miles. The general Width of the River all this Day is about three Quarters of a Mile, or rather leſs.

4th. About Noon eſpied the Suburbs of *New Orleans,* and at 2 o'Clock came abreaſt of the City on the Eaſtern Side of the River, in an Iſland formed by the *Miſſiſippi* and the
Bayoue

Bayoue St. John. This City is the Refidence of *Don Miro* a *Spanifh* Viceroy, and Emporium of *Louifiana* and the *Indian* Territories dependent thereon—It lies in almoft an exact Square. The Streets which are wide, and fome of them well paved with Brick, interfect each other at right Angles. The public Buildings are capacious and elegant. The private Houfes generally neat and commodious. Both Defcriptions lie compact and cover a Space of Ground of rather more than Half a Mile fquare. As the Situation of *New Orleans* was originally Nothing more than an extenfive Morafs, and fubject to the Inundation of the *Miffifippi*, it became neceffary to exclude the Water, by conftructing Dikes from about ten to fifteen Feet in Height, and double that Meafure in Width. The fteady Exertions of many Hands were, and ftill are employed in the Bufinefs; notwithftanding which, the Dikes are fometimes broken through, and confiderable Damage fuftained by the Influx of Water into their Cellars, Gardens and lower Rooms.

Along a fpacious Canal from the *Bayoue St. John*, to the Weftern Entrance of the City, both Fifh and Fowl of every Kind in great Abundance are brought to their Market;

ket ; which is alfo well fupplied with frefh Meats from various other Quarters.

April 7th.   The *French* and *Spanifh* Subjects of *Louifiana*, are ftrict *Romanifts*, and therefore, enthufiaftically fond of Pageantry in their religious Feftivals.   This I can avouch from a Proceffion of Yefterday, when a crucified Redeemer was crucified afrefh, in being reprefented like a Felon, in the Habiliment of a *Jefuit*.   The Virgin-Mother was drefs'd out *a-la-mode de Paris* ; and Traitor *Judas*, for political Reafons, appeared in the Regimental Uniform of a *Spanifh* Soldier, under Sentence of Death, for having divulged the Counterfign to the Enemy in Confideration of a *Bribe*.

In this Proceffion, I obferved a young *Kentuckean* who had been educated in all the Strictnefs of Prefbyterianifm, from which he had apoftatized, and embraced Anabaptifm and Methodifm, which he highly honoured, by ufing each Profeffion alternately, as Hypocrify might fuggeft.   He was prefented with a waxen Candle, which he devotionally received ; and, like the Knight of the woeful Countenance, joined the cheating and the cheated Throng.

The

On the Morning of the Proceffion, I planted myfelf near the Door of the Monaftry, and had a faint Glimpfe of the *Nuns* whilft they were adjusting their Capuchins. The Monaftery is near the Centre of the Town, and remarkable only for its Length, which if I miftake not, is about Two Hundred Feet. The Hospital is fituate in the Weftern Edge of the City, where Nothing interrupts its Ventilation from the Eaft, South and North ; but unfortunately, as if intended to banifh Chearfulnefs from its Manfions, the Priefts have laid off a Burial Ground, which is enclofed on one Side by the Front Wall of the Building. The Chapel is in a ruinous State, and will not be repaired—A new one is erecting, to which, all the internal Decorations of the Old will be transferred.

Don Andrea, a *Catalan*, arrived in *New Orleans* about Twenty Years ago :

" *Propt on a Staff, deform'd with Age and Care,*
" *And hung with Rags that flutter'd in the Air.*"

For ten Years paft he hath been the richeft Subject in *Louifiana* or either of the *Floridas*. About three Years fince, he got difgufted with his Lady, againft whom he prayed and obtained a Divorce *a Vinculo Matrimonii*, and a Difpenfation from the Archbifhop of *Toledo,*

ledo, Primate of *Spain* and great Chancellor of *Caſtile*, for an inceſtuous Marriage with her younger Siſter. To procure an Indulgence of this Kind, required a conſiderable Largeſs from the Coffers of the old Mammomiſt. He is now erecting to the Glory of *God*, and in Atonement of his Raſcalities a ſuperb Church and Hoſpital. No Doubt when theſe ſhall be completed, but that he will be reminded by the Prieſts, who will know how to excite the Paſſions of Hope and Fear ; that ſome other expiatory Acts remain, and which he is indiſpenſably bound to perform, under no leſs Penalty than of having his Soul everlaſtingly damned in the liquid Flames of Hell-fire. To ſoothe his Vanity, his Name and Pious Deeds, will be enſculptured over the Front Doors and other Parts of the Buildings.

> " *Who builds a Church to God, and not to Fame,*
> " *Will never mark the Marble with his Name.*"
>
> Pope.

The *Orleanois* as I obſerved before, are ſtaunch Romaniſts, and conſider People of all other religious Denominations as Heretics, and to whom they not long ſince denied chriſtian Burial. Their Cuſtom was to throw the Body of the deceaſed, unſhrouded and

and uncoffin'd into the *Miſſiſippi*. Not many Years ago, an *Engliſhman*, by the Name of *Howard*, influenced by Motives to Humanity, purchaſed about four Acres of Land in the Suburbs of the City, and generouſly aſſigned it as a Burial Ground for *Proteſtants* and *Strangers*. I ſaw the Interment of a Corpſe. The Grave was about four Feet deep. The Water roſe within ten Inches of the Surface, and the Coffin was ſunk down with heavy Stones.

Private Adventurers from *New-York*, *Philadelphia* and *Baltimore*, carry on a tolerable Trade at this Place—They have an Advance of Cent per Cent on their Goods, which are neverthelefs cheaper than *Spaniſh* Importations. I could not aſcertain what Impoſt is exacted here, but imagine it to be about fifteen per Cent ad Valorem.

During my Continuance in *New Orleans*, I got acquainted with the celebrated Major *Fairlamb*, whoſe Name will be memorable from the Circumſtance of his having in the Courſe of the laſt War, with only Sixty-three Men in a Blockhouſe, withſtood and repulſed General *Wayne*'s whole Brigade. He is now Surveyor-General for the King of *Spain* in *Louiſiana*. I had an ironical Meſ-

ſage

E

fage from him to General *Wayne*, whom I had not the Pleafure of Seeing, in my Route through *Georgia*.

May 16th. Went on Board the Governor's Packet at the *Bayoue St. John*, bound to *Mobille* and *Penfacola*. In this *Bayoue* I counted Seventy-three Alligators, which the Eye could eafily take in at one View. The Tail part of this Animal yields a very nutritious Food, and on which, the *Indians* and *Negroes* voracioufly englut and gormandize. They are eafily killed with a Rifle Ball, difcharged about an Inch below the Eyes—All other Parts except the Belly, are clothed with impenetrable Scales. The ufual Length of thofe I faw, were from fix to ten Feet; though fome few are now and then feen, which meafure upwards of Twenty Feet. I was informed by an intelligent *Spaniard* that they are of the fame Genus with the Crocodile on the River *Nile*, many of which he had critically examined in the Courfe of his late Travels. On Board of this Veffel were Paffengers, ten miferable *Spaniards* and a poor *Negro*, laden with combrous Chains, whofe inceffant clangous Sounds, united with Heartrending Groans, tranfpierced my Ear, and fadden'd all my Soul. They were under the Care of an Enfign, whofe Feelings appeared

to

to be equally wounded with my own. Their Fate will be confinement in a Prifon Ship, till they, with many others, now in the *Calliboufe* at *Mobille*, reach their ten Years gloomy Abode in the Copper Mines, where they will be excluded from the Light of Heaven, and drag out a miferable Exiftence under the Iron Rod of ruthlefs Oppreffion, in hard and unremitting Labour. Providence was kind to thefe poor Wretches. At times they were chearful, and by no Means feemed to anticipate the fubterraneous Horrors which await them.

17th. Arrived at *Penfacola*, the Metropolis of *Weft Florida*. There are fome elegant Buildings in this Place, particularly the Palace, Barrack and Chapel. Whilft *Penfacola* was in Poffeffion of the *Britifh* Government, it was under an excellent Police, and wore a very different Afpect from what it now does ; a great Part of the Town being in a ruinous State. There is but one Tavern for the Accommodation of *Americans* and Foreigners, and its Rates are enormoufly high. Their Market is well fupplied with aquatic Productions of every Species peculiar to the Climate, and with flight Induftry, might vie with Northern Markets in Mutton, Beef and Pork, with the fuperiour and additional Ad-

E 2

vantage

vantage of Venifon. Perennial Fruits of all Kinds, except Apples, they have in the greateft Profufion.

Don Arturo O'Neil, Governor of this Province informed me, that during an eleven Years Refidence in *Penfacola*, he had never experienced a Moment's Sicknefs ; and that all the Citizens enjoyed uninterrupted Health, except the *Spanifh* Garrifon; whofe Mode of Living, will, at all Times, and in all Places, be productive of complicated Difeafes. Inordinate Ufe of Ardent Spirits and bad Wine, fuperadded to high feafoned Meats and promifcuous Intercourfe with lewd Women, will diforder any the moft robuft Habit of Body.

Immediately back of the Town is a delightful Acclivity, from whence iffue many bubbling Fountains of wholefome, pleafant Water, filtrated through the Sand which conftitutes the Hill. The upper and lower *Creek* Nation trade to this Place, where they are uniformly impofed upon by a Mr. *Panton*, who hath monopolized their Trade. The poor *Indians* barter their Deer Skins at fourteen Pence Sterling per Pound, for Salt at nine Shillings Sterling per Bufhel. *Panton* is Part Owner of the Salt Works in the Ifland

Iſland of *Providence*, and has it brought to *Penſacola* in his own Bottoms, at the Average Expence of about three Pence per Buſhel. I think his Goods at *Mobille*, *Penſacola* and St. *Marks*, are generally vended at about Five Hundred per Cent on their prime Coſt.

After having ſpent about a Week in *Penſacola*, experiencing greater Civilities from his Lordſhip than my moſt ſanguine Expectations could have depicted, I departed with an Eſcort of eleven *Indians*, to whom I was introduced by the Governor, as an *Engliſh* Ambaſſador Incog. This ludicrous Title I endeavoured to ſupport, during my Paſſage, through a Wilderneſs of Three Hundred Miles, by aſſuming wiſe Catonia Looks, big with momentous and myſtical Concerns. My mock Gravity forſook me whenever I drew over the Stage of Imagination, a Groupe of old Acquaintance viewing me in my new and farcial Capacity of Ambaſſador from the Court of *London* to an *Indian* Emperor.

My *Indian* Companions (from their Conduct I judge) were much pleaſed with various Parts of my Dreſs, which they would in my Preſence, try on and pull off, and pack away in their Budgets ; always remembering

to

to make a Bow and fay, "Tank you Sir," which extorted from me a Nod of Confent, with the Addition of, *You're welcome Gentlemen.* The very ample Stock of Rum, Wine, &c. with which the Governor had fupplied me, was, with like Ceremony by them, and other Parties which we frequently met, confumed in about three Days. In about 20 Miles from *Penfacola* we reached the *Indian* Boundary, no Part of their Territory ever approaching nigher than that Diftance to the Sea-board. Notwithftanding the natural Sterility of Soil from *Penfacola* almoft to the *Tallipoofee* River, the Long-leaf'd *Pine*, *Hickory*, *Oak*, *Poplar*, and *Walnut* Trees grow to their ufual Height, and protect from the fcorching Rays of the Sun the tall and tender Grafs; among which Plants, Shrubs and Flowers of variegated Hue, and of rare medicinal Virtues, are interfperfed; a Catalogue of which, fhall be fubjoined to fome future Page.

June 1ft. Arrived at General *M'Gillivray*'s Houfe, fituate on the *Coufee* River, about 5 Miles above its Junction with the *Tallipoofee*, which forms the *Alabama*, whofe Confluence with the *Tombigbee* forms the Bay of *Mobille*. —At the Mouth of *Mobille* River, which empties into the Bay, is a Town of fimilar Name, of which, having only a tranfient

View

View, I shall not attempt a Defcription; but only obferve that it is garrifon'd, and from its Locality, muft 'ere long furpafs *Penfacola*, in Population, Trade and Buildings.—The fertile Grounds upon all the above laft mentioned Rivers are fettled and fettling by Corn, Hemp and Tobacco-Makers, who will have a nearer and better Navigation to *Mobille* than to *Penfacola*—add to this the Peltry-Trade, which will trebly exceed that of *Tenfacola*, as being nearer to the Hunting-Grounds from whence they may have Water-Carriage, except at one or two places, where a very flight Portage will be neceffary.

On my Arrival at *M'Gillivray*'s where my *Indian* Efcort left me, I was informed that he had juft gone to his upper Plantation, on the fame River, about 6 Miles diftant from his prefent Refidence: Thither I impaired in Company with his Nephew, who fupplied me with an *Indian*'s ftray Horfe.—We had not ridden far, before we unfortunately met the Owner, who, with a menacing Countenance and *fans Ceremonie*, feized the Bridle and ordered me to difmount immediately.——An Hour's Walk brought me to the Place, where the General was fuperintending fome Workmen in the Erection of a Log Houfe embellifhed with dormer Windows, on the very

Spot

Spot where his Father refided whilft a Trader in the Nation. Here are fome tall old Apple-trees planted by his Father, which make a venerable Appearance, tho' greatly obftruct the Profpect to and from his rural humble Palace.

He received me with Franknefs and Civility; modeftly enquired into my Bufinefs, and promifed every Affiftance in his Power towards my Accomodation, whilft I fhould think proper to make his Houfe my Home:—Do they order Things better in France? This Gentleman to Appearance is at leaft Five and Forty, tho' in Fact only Thirty-two Years of Age—Diffipation marked his juvinile Days, and fapped a Conftitution originally delicate and feeble.—He is fubject to an habitual Head-Ach and Cholic, notwithftanding which his Temper is placid and ferene, and at Intervals of Eafe quite joyous. He poffeffes an Atticifm of Diction aided by a liberal Education, a great Fund of Wit and Humour, meliorated by perfect good Nature and Politenefs.—His Lady confidering the Mode of Education to which fhe was fubjected in the early Part of Life, is a Model of Prudence and Difcretion; and could her Complexion, which is *olive*, be commuted for the lovely Tints of *red* and *white*, fhe would be

" *A Woman lovelieft of the lovely Kind,*
" *Perfect in Body, and complete in Mind.*"

By

By this Lady the General has two lovely Children, *Alexander* and *Elizabeth*. They fpeak the Englifh Tongue as well as Children of a fimilar Age ufually do among us.

He has a confiderable Number of Negroes at his different Plantations, probably more than Fifty, and common Report fays, double that Number in the Spanifh Weft-India Iflands; as alfo large Stocks of Horfes, Hogs, and horned Cattle. Two or three White Men fuperintend their refpective Ranges, and now and then collect them together in Order to brand, mark, &c: This they effect by giving them a little Salt in their Inclofures. His Table fmokes with good fubftantial Diet, and his Side-board difplays a Variety of Wines and ardent Spirits.—The General encourages his People in all Kinds of gymnaftic Exercifes; his Motives for which may be eafily conjectured—He invited me to a Ball-Match, about 10 miles from his Houfe, between two Townfhips. Sixty-two alert young Fellows were felected from each Town. The Goals were fet up about a Quarter of a Mile apart, near the Center of an extenfive Campaign or Praire.— They confift of two blazed Saplings fixed in the Ground about 10 Feet afunder at either End, thro' which every Time either Party throws the Ball with their Rackets, they are

F   entitled

entitled to count one—The Number of the Game is arbitrary.—Midway between the Goals, the Ball is thrown up alternately by two old Men, who are mutually chofen by the contending Parties to decide, all Controverfies which may arife in the Courfe of the Game—Upon throwing up the Ball a violent Struggle enfues between the Parties which fometimes lafts 8 or 10 Minutes, before either Side can give it a caft; and when they do, there are others of their Opponents ready to intercept and give it an adverfe Direction.—On this Game Property to a very confiderable Amount is generally rifqued, confifting of Broaches, Bracelets, Gorgets, Medals, Paints, Arms and Ammunition piled up in a pyramidical Form. Sometimes their whole Family Stock of Food and Raiment is hazzarded.—A diflocated Joint or fractured Bone is not uncommon: Suffer what they may, you'll never fee an angry Look or hear a threatening Word among them.

The Players deveft themfelves of all their Cloaths, except their Flaps. They ingenioufly difguife themfelves with various coloured Paints and affume the Semblance of Rattle-Snakes entwin'd about their Legs Thighs and Arms; whilft fpiral Streaks of *red, white, black* and *blue*, alternately adorn their other Parts.—

The

The vanquished Party immediately upon the Conclusion of the Game, betake themselves to their Heels, in Order to avoid the Scoffs and Ridicule of their boastful Conquerors.

Our President, whilst *M'Gillivray* was in *New-York*, complimented him with a Selection of elegantly gilt bound Books ; as also with the Golden Epaulet which he had worn throughout the War.   The latter *M'Gillivray* considers as a great Honor conferred upon him ; and therefore, says, he "*prizes it far above Rubies and much fine Gold.*"   He receives annual Presents from his Father in *Scotland*, which he modestly displays to his Friends, saying, those I received from my natural, these from my political and adopted Father.

The Reader is here presented with a Specimen of *M'Gillivray's* epistolary Composition, extracted from two Letters addressed to Messrs. *Boyd & Ker* of *Richmond*, and to Mr. *Collin Douglass* of *Manchester*, both written in Haste, and in a Circle of many Chieftains, whose Garrulity would have confused any other Man than *M'Gillivray*.

"*Little Tallisee, Upper Creek Nation, 5th June*, 1791.
"DEAR SIRS,

"MR. Pope having called here on his Way Home, I embrace the Opportunity of making you my warmest "Acknowledgements, for the polite Attention which you "were pleased to shew to me, when I had the Pleasure of "being with you last Summer.   " The

" The Indifpofition with which I was attacked at New-
" York, rendered me unable to return by the Route I had
" promifed myfelf, and induced me to make a Paffage by Sea,
" neceffary to eftablifh my Health.

" In the Hurry of fetting out at an early Hour from Rich-
" mond, I forgot to difcharge a fmall Account I owed you ;
" Not recollecting the exact amount ; but imagine it to be
" within the Compafs of a Guinea ; I have given Col. Pope
" one to deliver to you on my Account.

" Wifhing you every Profperity, I remain
" Gentlemen, your very obliged
" Humble Servant,
" ALEXANDER M'GILLIVRAY."

" Mess'rs. BOYD & KER.

" *Upper Creek Nation*, 8*th June*, 1791.

" DEAR SIR,

" THE Bearer Col. Pope being on his Return Homeward,
" from a Weftern Tour, and learning that he lives
" in your Neighbourhood, I embrace the favourable Oppor-
" tunity to make you and your very accomplifhed Lady my
" warmeft Acknowledgements, for the polite and friendly
" Attention fhewn me when on my Tour laft Summer.

" The Effects of a fevere Indifpofition at New-York rendered
" me incapable of returning by the Route in which I came ;
" and after a tolerable Paffage of Fifteen Days, we landed at
" St. Mary's in Georgia.

" I felt great Regret that it was not in my Power to make
" my Refpects in Perfon, to the hofpitable and friendly
" Gentlemen of Manchefter and Richmond : but be affured
" I fhall long remember them———And " *Sweet Jim of Aber-*
" *deen*," ftill vibrates on my Ear.

" That you and your accomplifhed Lady may long enjoy
" Happinefs, and every Profperity, is the Wifh of

" DEAR SIR,
" Your moft obedient
" Humble Servant,
"ALEXANDER M'GILLIVRAY."

" COLLIN DOUGLASS, Esquire.

Having fpent an agreeable Time among the
upper *Creeks*, I took my Departure on the
General's Horfe, with his Overfeer as an Efcort to the Lower Towns of *Coweta, Broken-*
Arrow

Arrow and *Cuſſatee*. The two former lie on the Weſtern, and the latter on the Eaſtern Side of the *Chattahoutchee* River, which takes its Name from two *Indian* Words; *Chatta*, a Stone, and *Houtchee*, which ſignifies marked or inſcribed. This Stone lies about 3 Miles above the *Coweta*, at the Rapids, covered over with hieroglyphic Inſcriptions, which the preſent Race do not underſtand. On the Weſtern Side of the River, upon the low Grounds of the *Cuſſatees* is a Mount, on whoſe Summit are the evident Traces of a Parapet ſufficiently large to have contained one Thouſand Men. This Mount appears to have been the Work of Ages and of many Hands, being upwards of 600 Yards in Circumferrence at its Baſe, and about 100 Feet in perpendicular Height. On the Weſtern Side and immediately oppoſite to the Mount, are the Veſtiges of a very large and deep Intrenchment, thrown up in a circular Form by the Anceſtors of the preſent Race, as a Defence againſt a numerous Tribe of the *Seminolies*, whom the *Creeks* after a long and bloody Conteſt of 20 Years, extirminated, and re-peopled the deſerted Villages by ſlow Emigrations from their own victorious Tribes. This Event according to the oral Tradition of the *Creeks*, happened about *Ten Thouſand* Years ago, when they had a Giant-King of moſt ſtupendous Size, called *Billy Pig*, who in Times of *Dearth*, would ſtop the *Chattahoutchee* with his Foot, and divert the Current over all the neighbouring Fields: That the *Alligators* got offended at his Conduct, and begged their King to ſnap off his great Toe; the Loſs of which prevented him from damming up the Water any more with that Foot; and ſo he died of Grief, and was burried under the circular Mount already mentioned, coil'd up like a Rattle-Snake.

During my Tarriance at the lower Towns, I formed an Intimacy with the *Little King* of the *Broken Arrow*, who is friendly, communicative and intelligent. Through him, with the Aid of an Interpreter, I attempted to compoſe a ſmall Vocabulary of the *Creekiſh* Tongue, particularly of ſuch Words as moſt frequently occur in common Intercourſe. In the proſecution of this, I enquired of him what Appellation he had for God? he replied, *Sawgee Putchehaſſee*, which ſignifies the Giver and Taker of Breath: And pray with what Epithet is your Majeſty pleaſed to honor the poor old Devil? with Emotions of Contempt he replied; there is no Devil: God Almighty is too much of a Gentleman to keep bad Servants about him. Juſt at this Inſtant, his Majeſty received an Invitation to a Rum-
Drinking

Drinking, which in Oppofition to all my Dif-
fuafions, he refolved to honour with his Pre-
fence. This Rum-Drinking or Spewing-
Match was held in the public Square, conti-
guous to their Hot-Houfe; in one or other
of which Places, as the Seafon may require,
the *Wittenagemote* of the Diftrict affemble for
the Difcuffion of all Subjects, whether civil
or military, moral or divine. Here alfo they
hold their War Dances, difplay their Tro-
phies of War, and keep their annual Feftival
called the *Bufk*. This Feftival generally com-
mences about the middle of *July*, upon the
firft Difcovery of ripen'd Corn, and is the
grand Epocha of the *Creeks*. All the Male
Clafs who have attained the Age of Puberty,
religioufly abftain from all Intercourfe with
the other Sex, and every Kind of Suftenance,
except Water, for three Days; which from
the Cathartics and Emetics they then fwal-
low, are called the Days of Purgation. Thus
cleanfed from the Impurities of the former
Year, they extinguifh every Particle of Fire
throughout their Diftrict, and rekindle more
by the Friction of a round *Saffafras* Stick, in an
Augur Hole bored into a Piece of dry *Poplar*.
This Relighting of the Fire, is performed by
their Chief Prieft or *Sachim*, and communicated by Torches to the Mafter or Miftrefs

of

of each refpective Family. This done, a mul-
tifidous Mefs of new Corn, cooked over the
new Fire, is brought into the Centre of the
Square, and diftributed with great Formality
among the Guefts, agreeable to Seniority and
Rank, by old Men and Women deputed for
that Purpofe. When the Repaft is over, they
rife up with one Confent, and with many
ftrange Gefticulations and loud Shouts of *Indian* Triumph, dance down the Sun, Moon,
and Seven Stars. At the Clofe of almoft every
Day throughout the Year, about 15 or 20
principal Townfmen affemble in the Square,
for the Purpofe of giving or receiving the moft
recent Intelligence, whether foreign or do-
meftic, which if important, is reported to their
grand Council, and by them to the National
Affembly, whofe Decrees on the Occafion,
are generally ratified by their Emperor, who
has Power alfo of rejecting them.—The *Creeks*
confider Fornication as a *Faux Pas* or venial
Crime at moft: but Wo! to the Sons and
Daughters who commit Adultry: Vengeance
in a fwift Career purfues them and cannot be
appeafed, but by the corporeal Sufferance of
the Aggreffors. Upon a Detection of the
Crime, about 50 or 60 Perfons of each Sex,
repair to a Thicket, and fupply themfelves
with *Hickory* Clubs; this done, the Men de-

termine

termine upon the Meafure of Punifhment to be inflicted on the Woman and permit the Women to decide upon the Man's. They then feparate, brandifhing their Clubs; the Men in Queft of the Woman, the Women in Queft of the Man. The Adultrefs when found, is feized upon, and ignominioufly dragged into a Circle formed by the Men, who beat her with their Clubs till fhe can no longer ftand; and whilft extended on the Ground, the A-vengers proceed to dock her Hair, crop her Ears, and flit her Noftrils; of all this her Ina-morato, is made an unwilling Spectator, and fometimes an Agent; who, in Turn, fuffers a fimilar Difgrace in the Circle of the Women, his fair Dulcinea looking on. What I have here mentioned are the higheft Punifhments they ever inflict, even upon the moft atrocious Offenders.—Sometimes they difpenfe with cropping their Ears and flitting the Noftrils, and content themfelves, with giving the Of-fender a found Drubbing and a fhort *Dock* :— This Lenity was extended a few Days ago to a Mr. *Patrick Murphy*, who plead Juftification; alledging that he was a Foreigner, ignorant of their Ufages and Laws; that the Woman was no Chriftian, having never been *baptized*; and that not having the Fear of God before her Eyes; what he had done was altogether *accidental.*

GIf

If the Club Bearers ever relinquiſh, or lay down their Clubs through any Miſhap or Neceſſity; before they encircle the Objeƈt of their Vengeance, they dare not reſume them again, as it is preſumed, that it was ſo ordered by their God, in tender Mercy to the Delinquents, who are accordingly acquitted of that Offence.

Upon the Deceaſe of an Adult of either Sex, the Friends and Relations of the Decedent religiouſly colleƈt whatever he or ſhe held moſt dear in Life, and inter them cloſe by and ſometimes in their Owner's Grave. This pious Tribute to their Dead includes Horſes, Cows, Hogs and Dogs, as well as Things inanimate. A Girl of about 16 Years of Age died a few Days before I left the Nation. She had procured from a *Spaniſh* Officer at *Penſacola*, a likely Boar-Pig of the *Spaniſh* Breed, which ſhe brought Home, and cheriſhed in her Boſom, until he waxed ſtrong, and became an uſeful Member in his Generation. Now when her Brethren, and the young Men of the Land, perceived that the Damſel was dead; they aroſe up and purſued after the Boar and ſlew him. And a certain young Man of the Houſe of *Illeſenekaw* ſtood up in the Midſt of the Congregation, and ſaid; I will go unto my Lord the King and unto the Elders and Chief Men of the Land, and ſay unto them, Verily
the

the Big Boar of *Chattahoutchee* is flain; by
the Arrows of the Sons of *Ninewaw* is he
fallen! And they faid unto him Go: And he
departed and went unto the King, and unto
the Elders and Chief Men of the Land, and
reported all thefe Things; faying, Verily the
Big Boar of *Chattahoutchee* is flain, by the
Arrows of the Sons of *Ninewaw* is he fallen.
And when the King and the Elders and Chief
Men heared thereof, they drank ftrong Drink
and grew exceeding Wroth, faying; the Blood
of the Boar be upon the Head of thofe, who
have wrought this Evil in *Coweta*; for they
wift not that the Damfel was dead——This
extraordinary Circumftance extorted from me
an Epitaph on the Damfel and the Boar, who
are now Jointenants of one Grave.

> *Beneath this Turf a Woman,*
> *Lies burried with a Boar;*
> *Which to all Sows was common,*
> *As fhe to all Men, Whore.*

The *Creeks* regularly make a Burnt Offering of what they conceive to be the moft delicious Parts of every Animal taken in Hunt-
ing, before they prefume to tafte a Mouthful.
The Parts they commit to the Flames are
proportioned to the Size of the Animal, probably about 2 or 3 lb. from a *Buffalo*, and
ftill lefs in a regular gradation down to the
fmalleft Quadrupede, Fifh or Bird.   The

The *Creeks* like the *Otaheiteans* as mentioned in *Cook*'s Voyages, have a Cuſtom of *Tatowing* themſelves, and probably upon ſimilar Principles. The young and old of both Sexes undergo this Operation in Silence, and without the leaſt muſcular Diſtortion. I ſaw it performed upon a Child of 4 Years old, who when releaſed gave a Shout, and ſaid, now "*I'm a Man, and a Warrior too.*"

Thoſe who live in Townſhips are Tenants in Common of large extenſive Fields of Corn, Rice and Potatoes, which commonly lie on the fat low-Grounds of ſome River convenient to their Towns.

The Cultivation of the Soil and almoſt every domeſtic Drudgery are impoſed upon their Women, who are leſs prolific than ours ; probably owing to their hard Labour and exceſſively coarſe and ſcanty Diet. A long rainy Seaſon had rendered their Fields ſo quaggy that all Cultivation was impracticable ; they durſt not even venture to cut down the tall rank Weeds which towered above their Corn. In this general Diſtreſs an old Conjuror, of the Name of *Senetahawgo* ſtept forth into the Square, and thus harrangued the liſtening Crowd :

" Men & Warriors *of* Coweta, Broken-Arrow & Cuſſatee,

" THE great God of Thunder and Lightning and of Rain, who ſtands upon the aerial

Battle-

Battlements of Heaven, hath raifed his angry terrifonous Voice, and with the Lightnings flafhing from his Eyes, hath rent the Bofom of the Clouds! He hath hidden the Sun behind the Moon, and covered her Face with a Bear-Skin: With the Tails of numerous Beavers, he hath conceal'd the twinkling Stars! We have been Traitors to our God, to *Hippo ilk Meco*, to *Lauco Wafhington*! We have rejected the good Talk of *Hippo ilk Meco*, and liftened to the lying Talk of *Cherokees!* We have infringed the Treaty with *Lauco Wafhington* in ftealing Horfes from his Children! Our young Men refufe to hunt:—their Guns are rufty and their Hatchets dull! They fell their Horfes, Cloaths and filver Ornaments for Rum. Our Women laugh at us and refufe to work: they are Proftitutes and fuckle the Children of white Men! Our Men are worfe than the Excrement of Dogs or *Spaniards*:—Our Women viler than the Urine of *Pole-Cats* or the Vomit of *Buzzards*! For thefe Caufes are our Fields drenched by the angry Clouds of the Firmament.

When will the gladfome Rays of Sol return and deficcate our flooded Fields? Ah! never till in Duft and Afhes we repent, and forfake our evil Ways. Men and Warriors, let us confefs our Faults and amend our Manners;

and

and then *Sawgee Putchehaffee* will forgive us, and bid the Sun to fhew himfelf, and with a genial Warmth revive our drooping Corn.— My Sons, I'm very old and chilly ; the Marrow of my Bones is dry, and fcarcely creeps the Blood along thefe Veins, which once in rapid Currents flow'd—I want a Keg of Rum. —My Daughters, I have fafted for three Days and Nights, and invoked my God in your Behalf.—I am hungry as a *Wolf*.—I want to eat fome Hog and Hominy."

A plaintive dull Monoty conftitutes the vocal Mufic of the *Creeks*.   They are paffionately fond of inftrumental Mufic, particularly that of the Violin, to which like Perfons bitten by the *Turantula*, they will dance for feveral Hours without the leaft Intermiffion.

No People under Heaven are more attached to, or fwerve lefs from, the Cuftoms of their Anceftors than the *Creeks*.   Whether this Attachment originates in filial Piety, or in Ignorance I cannot determine: But as a Clue for Conjecture, let me relate their Mode of Cropping.

They plant their Corn in Holes at an unequal, tho' never greater Diftance than Tobacco Hills, from one another.   Twenty or thirty Grains are frequently thrown into an Hole
which

which produce as many earlefs Stalks, and which they will upon no Confideration fuffer to be thin'd. They fay a plough is nothing but a Horfe-trap, and therefore never ufe it, contenting themfelves with light Weeding Hoes, with which they barely fcalp the graffy Surface of their Fields. Their Inclofures are Fork and Rail Fences juft high enough to keep out horned Cattle. Whilft their Crops are in the Ground they tether out their Horfes, Hogs &c, to Trees, Stumps and Stakes. Tho' they have numerous limpid Streams of excellent Spring Water gufhing from their River Banks, yet like old *Seneca* they prefer the tepid Waters from their Creeks and Rivers. They fcarcely ever weed, hill, prime, top or fuccour their Tobacco, and always cut and cure it very green over a hafty blaft of Fire, as they do their *Killicanic* or *Sumac* Leaves, which when mixed with Tobacco, emit a moft delightful Odour from the Pipe. This Preparation of *Sumac* and *Tobacco*, the *Indians* conftantly fmoke, and confider as a fovereign Remedy in all cephalic and pectoral Complaints.

The *Creeks* in approaching the Frontiers of *Georgia*, always encamp on the right Hand fide of the Road or Path, affigning the left, as ominous, to the *Larvæ* or Ghofts of their departed Heroes who have either unfortunately

ly loft their Scalps, or remain unburied. The Ghoft of an Hero in either Predicament, is refufed Admittance into the Manfions of Blifs, and fentenced to take up its invifible and darkfome Abode, in the dreary Caverns of the Wildernefs; until the Indignity fhall be retaliated on the Enemy, by fome of his furviving Friends.

Agriculture among the *Creeks* is little underftood and lefs practifed.—I know of but one Man in the whole Nation, who poffeffes tolerable Induftry, and that is a private Citizen, called the *Bully*, who from a very humble Beginning hath accumulated an eafy Fortune, confifting of the following Species of Property, viz. Of Negroes, 16 Men, 19 Women and 26 Children. Of Horfes, 5 Studs, 32 Geldings, 127 Mares and 83 Colts. Of black Cattle, 19 Bulls, 58 Steers, 326 Cows, and 132 Calves. Of Hogs about 300 Head; befides Houfhold Furniture, Peltry and Store Goods, to a very confiderable Amount. Two likely young Wenches between the Ages of 15 and 20, are the only Children the *Bully* has, and from his advanced Age, its probable he will never encreafe the Number. It is faid the *Black Dog* is a Man of Property, tho' a moft egregious Sot and Sluggard.—I once faw his Majefty in a Puddle of his own Ex-

crement

ment and Urine, which attracted Swarms of *Spanish Flies* and *Beetles,* whose constant Buzz had lull'd him into sweet Repose. The Powers of their Kings appear to be very circumscribed and nearly on a Par with those of a common County Magistrate with us, the Limits of their respective Governments being sometimes confined to a single Township, or a Spot of Ground not more than Ten Miles Square. *M'Gillivray* who is perpetual Dictator, in Time of War subdelegates a Number of Chieftains for the Direction of all military Operations; and when the War concludes, they, in Compensation for their martial Atchievements, are invested by the Dictator with civil Authority which supersedes the hereditary Powers of their Demi-Kings.

June 29th. The *Little King* of the *Broken-Arrow* returned, and furnished me with the following Catalogue of *Indian* Words, with a literal Translation to each by Mr. *Darisoux*, Linguist to the *Lower Creeks.*

Sawgee Putchehasse, God, or the Giver and Taker of Breath.
Hippo ilk Meco, M'Gillivray, or the good Child King.
Honuntauchee, Do. or the great Man.
Chuloehawjo, the mad Lightwood.
Chuleetawbe, the dry Pine.
Mecohawjo, the mad King.
Sow a ki gee, Lie by his Side.
Cowawigee, Mr. Thomas Kerr, or the Little Partridge.
Illesenekaw, the Baboon.
Chulesenekaw, the mad Dog.
Ninewaw, lie in the Path.
Senetehawgo, wait for the Day.
Iuletiga, he escaped from his Enemy.
Miss Sukee,

H *Putchesua*

Putchefua, An axe,
Waweaw Nunnowaw, a Bull.
Chutkfacvu, a Bridle.
Hatchee, a Creek.
Atchee, Corn.
Hocuffee, a Child.
Etchoo, a Deer.
Toatloa, an Eye.
Ah Hiffee, my Friend.
Cappo tooka, an Hat,
Chatto, Iron.
Meco, a King.
Ocunna, Land.
Ifte Hatkee, a white Man.
Ifte Chautee, an Indian or red Man.
Iftee Lufte, a negro or black Man.
Hoakta, a Woman.
Stignee, an Owl,
Catcha, a Panter.
Chitloc, an Horfe.
Itchca, a Gun.
Slaufcau, a Knife.
Cappo, a Coat.
Cappo Lauco, a great Coat.
Chautee, Blood.
Stillipiga, a Moccofon or Shoe
Ittee, a tree.
Toatka, Fire.
Tofeena, Bacon.
Wawcaw Piffee, Milk.
Wawcaw Piffee Nehaw, Butter.
WawcawPiffee Tuckaliga, Cheefe
Tuckaliga, Bread.
Ockchaunfwaw, Salt.
Hafwaw, Penes.
Hafnilcaw, Tefticuli.

Chulua, Pudendum Muliebre.
Hiefka, Fœminam fubagitare.
Piffee, the Breaft.
Epha, a Dog.
Epha Hoakata, a Bitch.
Nawenffee, a Bear.
Chawcawcaw, a Goofe.
Futchu, a Duck.
Pinnua, a Turkey.
Ilklo, a Squirrel.
Fufwaw, a Bird.
Chofee, a Sheep.
Chofochee, a Hare or little Sheep
Wootcoo, a Racoon.
Suka, a Hog.
Suka Hatkee, an Opoffum or white Hog.
Telafo, a Town.
Ponunga, an Indian Talk.
Ninnce Hee Mattee? is this the Way?
Ifte na aftcha? where are you going?
Na aftcha Penfacola, I am going to Penfacola.
Ifte nata ifca? where did you come from?
Nata efca New Orleans, I came from New-Orleans.
Wee Hummec, Rum, or ftrong Water.
Fo in Chumba, a Bee, or a Fly in Sweetnefs.
Netta Haffee, the Sun.
Netlee Haffee, the Moon.
Cocheechumba, a Star.
Tuftaniga, a Warrior.

Telawgo Hatchee, Pea Creek, and *Chaulee Hatchee*, Red River from a Bay of great Extent between St. Marks and Penfacola.

Wee launco Hatchee, yellow water River, makes a large Bay in Sight of Penfacola.

Wee Luftee, black Water Creek, empties into yellow Water River.

Wee Hatkee, white Water Creek, and *Wee Cuffappee*, Cold Water Creek, empty into *Conakee Hatchee*, which forms the Bay of Penfacola.   Took

Took my Departure from the Nation in Company with a Mr. *John Turvin*, who in Courfe of the laft War, to efcape the Perfecution of the *Georgians*, fled for Protection to the *Britifh* Standard, where he continued till the Surrender of *St. Auguftine*, from whence he repaired to the *Creek* Nation, took a Wife, and commenced a Trader. He is a friendly honeft Man, though very irritable when he conceives the leaft Indignity offered to him. To footh his captious Temper which involved both him and me in frequent Difficulties, I had Recourfe to Adulation, fuch as, I'm furprifed Mr. *Turvin*, that a Gentleman of your good Senfe fhould condefcend to word it with fuch low-liv'd Wretches!—You, who have been educated in the *Britifh* Camp, among Officers of the firft Rank and Dignity!—Fie! Fie! For a Gentleman to put himfelf upon a Level with fuch Cattle!

June 30th. Late in the Evening we arrived at an old deferted *Indian* Village, fituate on the Banks of *Flint* River, near an Hundred Miles from *Chattahoutchee*, with which it unites, and empties into the Ocean 50 Miles South of *St. Marks.*—About 30 Families from the *Chattahoutchee* Townfhips are refettling this Place. The late Rains had forced the River out of its Banks and rendered

it

it impaſſable to Mr. *Turvin*'s Horſes which were loaded with Beaver-Skins. In this perplexity two young Fellows very opportunely came up and proffered their Aſſiſtance in the Conſtruction of a Raft, compoſed of the Timbers from the old Village Houſes.—When we had croſſed the Stream, they propoſed going with us as far as the fœderal Fort on the *Oconee*, to which we readily aſſented, and found them very tractable in rendering every poſſible Aid in ſimilar Predicaments.

July 2 Encamped on the Banks of *Ockmulga* about 30 Miles from *Flint*. Here alſo we had Recourſe to our *Indian* Friends for another Raft as well as a Shelter from a moſt violent Rain which was then deſcending. They ſoon conſtructed both; the former with dry Logs, the latter with the Bark of Pines.— *Ockmulga* unites with the *Oconee*, and forms the *Alatamaha* which empties into the Sea North of *St. Mary*'s River, and is navigable for Veſſels of 40 or 50 Tons Burthen 300 Miles from its Mouth. Late in the Evening arrived at, and continued on the Banks of the *Oconee*, which was impaſſible for two Days.—Here our Proviſſions were exhauſted, and *Turvin* and myſelf appeared like Men without Hope, having left all our Ammunition on the South Bank of the *Ockmulga* at our laſt Encampment

ment. We communicated our Diſtreſs and Misfortune to our *Indian* Friends. They ſmiled at our Perplexity, and without informing us of their Intentions, immediately took different Routes, and in about 3 Hours returned, one with an *Opoſſum*, the other with about a Peck of Turtle Eggs, on which we fared ſumptiouſly during our two Days Confinement.

July — Early in the Morning we diveſted ourſelves of all our Cloathing, and confined it on the Tops of the Beaver Packs; then each Man with one end of a long Rope tied round his Horſe's Neck, and holding the other in his left Hand, plunged into the Stream and ſwam to the oppoſite Shore. In this hazardous and voluntary Attempt we in ſome Meaſure imitated what Cæſar did through Accident and Love of Fame, when caſt away. Thus having braved *Oconee*'s rough, rocky, rapid Stream which was then upwards of 200 Yards in Width, we reſumed our Dreſs, mounted our Nags, and in 2 Hour's Time reached the Fœderal Fort on the Eaſtern Bank of the River, about 10 Miles below the Place where we croſſed, and 2 Miles below the Rock Landing. At the Fort I continued 4 Days; being invited by Major *Call*, Capt. *Rudolph*, Lieut. *Martin* and Enſign *Clay* to ſpend the Anni-

verſary

verſary of American Independence with them. The Rejoicings of the Day were uſhered in by the Diſcharge of Muſketry and Cannon under the Direction of ſkillful Officers in each Department, at whoſe Expenſe a genteel Dinner was provided under a ſpacious Booth; to the Participation of which, Ladies and Gentlemen from the Country were invited. Several ſentimental Toaſts ſuitable to the Celibrity of the Day were drank, and at 6 o'Clock the Company repaired to a large Room in Town and partook of an excellent Supper, after which, with the Introduction of Minuets, Cotillions and Country Dances, the Evening was cloſed to the entire ſatisfaction of all Parties. On this Occaſion Major *Call* with his uſual Politeneſs invited my two *Indian* Companions, who expreſſed a ſtrong Deſire to enliſt into our ſervice, in which they concluded that a Man might wear fine Cloaths and fare ſumptuouſly every Day. The Town lies about half a Mile below the Fort, and the Buildings at both Places, conſiſt of very rough, ſlight Materials, as if intended merely to anſwer a temporary Shelter for a few Sojourners The Citizens however like other Southern People, are indolent, luxurious, fond of gaudy Apparel and pompous Equipage. Hither the *Creek Indians*, ſince their late Treaty with Congreſs, bring their Peltry, Furs, &c. in Barter for

Weſt

West-India and European Goods to the almost entire Exclusion of their former Merchants at *Mobille*, *Penſacola* and *St. Marks.*——In Digging a Well at this Place near the River Bank, the Workmen diſcovered many Strata of white black and red friable Loam, which are appropriated to three ſeveral Uſes,viz: the white for Starch, the black for Soap and the red for common Paint. The latter Kind excited the Curioſity of an *Indian* ſo far, that I ſaw him induſtriouſly employed near an Hour, in the Collection of about a dozen Pounds which he carefully packed away in his Paint-bag.

July —. Took our leave of this Place at about 10 o'Clock, and by 4 in the Evening arrived at, and paſſed through *Waſhington*, a ſmall Townſhip ſituate on the South Side of *Oguechee* River, at the upper End of the Falls, and moved on to another little Town about a Mile below it on the North Side, at the mouth of the Falls. I had only a tranſient View of theſe little Towns, which appeared to have been very lately erected ; a Deſcription therefore cannot be expected. At Sunſet, encamped about half a Mile from the Road, convenient to a Spring, on whoſe little Stream, our Horſes met with moſt delightful tender virgin Cane. Here I undertook to teach *Turvin* the *Lord*'s Prayer, which he ſoon learned,

having

having, as he said, had some little Smattering
of it before he went to the *Creek* Nation and
married a damn'd Heathen.——After a short
Repose in order to avoid the sultry Heat of
Noon, we arose, collected our Horses, and
pursued our Journey till 10 o'Clock the next
Day, when we halted and refreshed ourselves
and Nags till 3. At 5 o'Clock we passed the
Battle Ground where *Turvin* had been de-
feated by the *Creeks*, previous to our War
with *Britain.* The Recollection of former
Disasters rendered him somewhat phlegmatic;
but when at 6 we came in Sight of the House
in which he had been born and raised to Man's
Estate, and from which he had been driven

> *His lab'ring Breast inton'd a sullen Moan,*
> " *And Melancholy mark'd him for her own.*"

What's the Matter my Friend, you appear to
be melancholy? Oh! no Nothing, in particular:—I was thinking about some Parts of
the *Lord*'s Prayer. What Parts my Friend?
Why, that Part where it says "*as we forgive
them that trespass against us,*" its very good I
agree, but by *G—d* I don't think it will ever
be in my Power to comply with it.

Encamped within 15 Miles of *Augusta*, the
Metropolis of *Georgia,* and entered it early
the next morning.—Here my Friend *Turvin*

and

and I feparated, with mutual Expreffions of Regret, and folemn Affurances of lafting Friend-
fhip, and future Remembrance. He wifhed me
Health, Peace and Competence, and advifed
that whenever I fhould encamp in the Woods,
always to raife a good Fire, and fleep with my
Feet next to it. I wifhed him the like, and
recommended to his particular Attention the
Lord's Prayer, as the beft Directory that was
ever given to man.

The Soil, from *Penfacola* to *Augufta*, except
upon the Water Courfes where it is very fertile
wears the gloomy Face of uniform Sterility; tho'
being in a mild Region, is more Productive
than Ground of a fimilar Appearance in *Virginia.*—I was much pleafed with *Augufta* and
its high level Situation, but more fo with her
Citizens and the reputable Families in its Vicinage. Previous to my Arrival here I was
told by common *Fame*, that a great propor-
tion of them confifted of infolvent *Refugees*
from the northern States : but this is not the
only Inftance in which her Ladyfhip hath di-
viated from the Line of Truth and Candour.
Influenced by fome Nabobs in the *Modern
Colchis*, fhe hath alfo mifreprefented the whole
State of *Georgia*, together with all Perfons and
Things whatfoever, unto her belonging or in
any wife appertaining.

I

A

A wonderful Spirit for Building feems to have permeated every Rank and Clafs of People in and about this Place—A fine elegant Bridge of fuperior Strenth to any of its Size I ever faw, ftretches itfelf over the noble River *Savannah*, right abreaft of the Town, where it is navigable for Veffels of 50 or 60 Tons Burthen. The Bridge, together with many fine Houfes now erected and erecting here and in its Neighbourhood, do honor to *Augufta*, which will e're long vie with, if not eclipfe the former Seat of Government, in Buildings, Population, Trade and Commerce.—The *Auguftians* are remarkable for their Generofity and Politenefs, the Effects of which, I as a Stranger particularly experienced, at the Hands of two profeffional Gentlemen, Meffrs *Smelt* & *Williamfon*.——During my Continuance in this Neighbourhood, I paid a Vifit to his Excellency *William Telfair*, the prefent Governor of the State. He appeared to be a worthy honeft Man, endowed with plain good Senfe and great Simplicity of Manners. I am told that he is an Encourager of Agriculture and Mechanics, a good Moralift and bounteous Benefactor to the meritorious Poor and Indigent. After having fpent an agreeable Time at this Place, in the Society of both old and new Acquaintance, I proceeded down the River in a long Keelbottomed decked Boat, laden with 72

Hogfheads

Hogfheads of Tobacco, and feveral Thoufand Pounds Weight of various Kinds of Peltry, &c. This Boat had a decent Cabin fufficiently large for the Accommodation of the Captain and myfelf.

Juft below *Augufta* large extenfive Corn and Tobacco Fields commence, and from their Luxuriance of Growth, evince the amazing Fertility of Soil. On *Beech* Ifland and the Plantations of Meffrs *Bugg* and *Watkins*, I faw Cornfields of equal, if not fuperior Growth and Production, to the beft Spots in *Kentuckey*. On the 4th Day of our Paffage from *Augufta*, we anchor'd abreaft of *Ebenezer*, an old inconfiderable and declining Village, fituate on an high commanding Bluff, on the *Georgian* Side, from whence runs off a great Extent of level, tho' very fandy, piney barren Land—Here the *Britifh* Troops, whilft in Poffeffion of *Savannah* in 1779, eftablifhed a Garrifon of about 1500 Men, aided by a good Train of Artillery, ftrong Fortifications and deep Intrenchments, which however were no Impediment to the rapid Career of General *Wayne*, at the Head of his victorious Myrmidons.

At Break of Day weighed Anchor and proceeded down to a Col. *M---e*'s on the North Side of the River, in Order to land fome Dry Goods for a neighboring Gentleman. Previ-

ous

ous to my Arrival at his Houſe, the Captain had given me a particular Detail of his punitory Inflictions, on the Tories and others during the laſt War, all which he carried on under the ſpecious Pretext of his being a Whig-Officer in the *American* Service; tho' in Fact nothing more than a common Free-booter. I ſhall ever remember the Voice and patibulary, *Cain*-like Countenance of the Man, when the Captain introduced him to me. Tho' he is very uxorious of his preſent Spouſe, and tender of her Offspring, yet common Report does not heſitate to ſay, that he diſpatched his former Wife and only Son, by a Bowl of ſtrong and deadly Poiſon, which he impoſed upon them as a Doſe of *Indian* Phyſic.

" A Rugged Wight the worſt of Brutes this Man
" On his own Fellow-Creatures ruthleſs prey'd :
" The ſtrongeſt he, the weakeſt over-ran
" And o'er each Band of Brother-Robbers ſway'd ;
" For Guile and ruffian Force were all his Trrde :
" His Life a Scene of Rapine, Want and Woe ;
" Swift as an Indian Arrow Blood to ſhed
" And cauſe the Orphan's, Widow's Tears to Flow."

—OR THUS:—

1

Dame Nature once produc'd a Dunce,
    Her plaſtic Art to ſhew,
And o'er his Head, replete with Lead,
    A brazen Helmet threw.

2

With ſolid Block from Mountain Rock,
    Hew'd out with little Art,
She tho't the beſt, to fill his Cheſt,
    And repreſent a Heart.

Thus

3
Thus Head and Heart, she did impart,
    Adapted to the Size.
Of this huge Breast, who stands confest,
    A Bug-bear to our Eyes.

4
His Wife and Son, he first seiz'd on,
    And soon depriv'd of Breath;
His tortur'd Slaves next found their Graves,
    And seal'd their Woes in Death.

5
The Tory Herd next felt his Sword,
    Distain'd with Human Gore;
And heard the Cry of Traitor die,
    Beneath the Hand of M---e.

July 20th.   Early in the Morning weighed Anchor, and took a final Adieu of this Son of Iniquity.—Before the dread Tribunal of *Almighty God* he must e're long appear, and receive his final Doom.......May the *Lord* have Mercy on his Soul!.....At Noon we passed a small and almost depopulated Town, on the North Side of the River, called *Purisburg*, which was once to *Savannah*, what *German-Town* is now to *Philadelphia*. Late in the Evening of this Day, our Pilot run our Vessel aground, opposite to the Seat of the late Major General *Greene*, where we continued until 4 o'Clock P. M. of the succeeding Day, when with Difficulty we got afloat, by the Assistance of the General's Slaves,

Here begin on both Sides of the River very extensive Fields of Corn, Rice and Indigo, convenient to which are Mills, Vats, &c. to

manufac-

manufacture the Produce:——but when I turn my View toward the numerous Herds of poor miserable Slaves, whose Powers of Body are worn down amidst Stripes and Insults, in clearing Woods and draining Marshes, my very Soul revolts and sickens at the Thought.

Many and sharp the num'rous Ills
Inwoven with our Frame!
More pointed still we make ourselves,
Regret, Remorse and Shame.
And Man, whose Heav'n-erected Face
The Smiles of Love adorn,
Man's Inhumanity to Man
Makes countless Thousands mourn!
See yonder poor o'er-labour'd Wight
So abject, mean, and vile,
Who begs a Brother of the Earth,
To mitigate his Toil;
And see his lordly *Fellow-Worm*
The poor Petition spurn
Unmindful, tho' a weeping Wife
And helpless Offspring mourn!
Oh Death! the poor Man's dearest Friend,
The kindest and the best:
Welcome the Hour my aged Limbs
Are laid with thee at Rest!
The Great, the Wealthy fear thy Blow,
From Pomp and Pleasure torn;
But oh! a blest Relief to those
That weary-laden mourn. *Burn's Poems.*

From this Place to *Savannah*, the Eye is delighted with a continued Succession of beauteous Farms and elegant Buildings, inhabited by gay and liberal Proprietors, who in general appear to be of French Extraction.—Came abreast of the City about 8 o'Clock at Night, and altho' denied the Light of Moon or Star,

yet

yet a tall white fandy Bluff attiguous to the public Wharf, ferved as a Pharos to direct our Veffel fafely into Port.

Early the next Morning took Breakfaft, and engaged Lodgings at the City Coffee Houfe, and then fauntered till 10 o'Clock thro' the moft public Parts of the City, in order to fee, or be feen by, fome old Friend or Crony, who might probably be engaged upon a fimilar and equally important Bufinefs with myfelf. To my great Joy, the firft Perfon that faluted me was Col. *Jofeph Haberfham*, a Gentleman who in the Courfe of the laft War, had been a *Refugee* in the County of *Amherft*, where I then refided, and got acquainted with him.—He is a Gentleman of ftrict Honor and Integrity, a fafe Companion, and an eafy Friend, and tho' a Mortal, he cannot be altogether exempt from the Failings of Humanity, yet few and trivial as they are, they always ' *lean to Virtue's Side.*' By this Gentleman I was introduced to General *M'Intofh*, with whom I had been formerly acquainted, whilft on his Way to join the grand Army in the North. As an Officer he is too generally known to require any Encomium from my Pen ; but as a private Citizen is a moft excellent Model for the State. He is defcended from a very antient Family in *Scotland*. His Father who was a famous

Chieftain

Chieftain of a numerous Highland Clan, and remarkable for his Valour, and that rare Virtue in a Soldier, called Temperance, fell in Battle, whilft our Hero was yet a Minor, and bequeathed thofe Virtues to his Son, with an Injunction on him to fettle in *America* as foon as he fhould attain the Age of 21. His Mother whofe Chriftian Name was *Fortune* did not long furvive her Hufband. On her Death-bed, fhe called our Hero to her (for he was her favorite Son) and thus addreffed him :—" My Son the Patrimony which my honoured Hufband and your valiant Father left you, may be of Service to you, in the *Hurly Burly* Scenes of bluftering War, it is therefore my Requeft, that you never part with them :—but as when you come to be old, you may exchange the Army for the peaceful Walks of Life, I here deliver into your Poffeffion for a Beginning, all my Dower confifting of two faithful Hand-maids named *Induftry* and *Frugality*—Take them my Son, and ufe them well—they'll be of Service to you, whether you go to *America* or continue here ; tho' my Advice is to obey your Father's laft Requeft."—Bleffed with a vigorous Conftitution and a virtuous Education, our Hero croffed the *Atlantic* and fettled in the State of *Georgia*, bringing along with him his paternal and maternal Legacies. By Means of the former he rofe to high Preferment

in

in the United States Army; and by the latter hath accumulated an almoſt immenſe and princely Fortune.

In this Place I ſpent 3 Days, chiefly at the Houſes of the two laſt mentioned Gentlemen. Being much relaxed by Fatigue and Heat of Weather, I declined taking ſuch an accurate View of the City, as I at firſt intended. It is however happily ſituated for both foreign and internal Trade, as verging on the Atlantic to the Eaſt, and lying about Midway on the inland Navigation, which extends from *Charleſton* to *St. Mary*'s River, the Southern Extremity of the United States.

Savannah is, and ever will be, a Place of Opulence, ſo long as human Nature ſhall require Food and Raiment, or, Commerce ſpread her Canvaſs to the Wind.

July — About 2 o'Clock P. M. went on Board a large Packet Schooner, bound to *Charleſton*, and commanded by a Captain *Roſs*, in Company with Major *Butler*, a Congreſſional Senator, Mr. —— a *Charleſton* Merchant and Miſs —— of *Savannah*. In this Company I promiſed myſelf a pleaſant Paſſage enlivened with agreeable Converſation, in which however I was miſerably diſappointed; for no ſooner had we put to Sea, than ſqually Wea-

K

ther

ther and adverfe Winds arofe, and fo toft and rock'd our Veffel, that "we reeled to and fro and ftaggered like drunken Men, and were at our Wit's End."—In this Situation we continued till 10 o'Clock the following Day. The Agitation of the Veffel brought on a violent Sea ficknefs upon all the Paffengers except myfelf, and lafted with little Intermiffion, till we made the wifhed for Port of *Charlefton*—Between the Paroxifms of the Major's Qualms, I found him to be a lively converfable Gentleman, poffeffed of a great Fund of Wit, found Judgment, and good Breeding.——The laft Morning of our Paffage, I faluted the Merchant with, a good Morning to you Sir, how does Mr. —— find himfelf to day? Why Sir; I have caft up my Accounts over and over again, and find myfelf, upon ftriking a Balance, a better Man by an Hundred Per Cent, than I was this Time Yefterday, He! He! He! And pray how does Mifs —— find herfelf? *I thank you Sir, I'm inclin'd to believe I think I feel a little better at the* Stummick.

Auguft 1ft. Entered *Charlefton* about two o'Clock P. M. and immediately repaired to *M'Crady's* Hotel, which I had been told was, and found to be fuperior to any other in the City, whether for its Accommodations, the Civility of its Mafter, or, the amazing Concourfe

courfe of polite People from all the other States who frequent it. At this Hotel General *Wafhington* on his late Vifit through the Southern States took up his Refidence, and during which Perfons of all Ranks vied with each other in paying every Homage to him, which Gratitude could excite, and fplendid Tables, Garb and Equipage atteft.

The Situation of *Charlefton*, the Character of her Citizens and the Nature of her Police fit her for Trade and Commerce, which however are not driven to that Extent as is obfervable in fome Northern Towns which do not poffefs the third Part of her Opulence. The Topography of this City, is too generally known to require any Defcription from my Pen. I fhall therefore only obferve that in Point of Profpect, it eclipfes all other Cities in the Union and is inferior to only Three in Size, Wealth, Population, Trade and Elegance of Buildings. Her Citizens are a gay, luxurious People, fond of Drefs and pompous Equipage, in which they give the Ton to *Augufta* and *Savannah*, who are moft excellent Copyifts. Was the young *Phaeton* of this State with his fervile Imitators, to repair to *Charlefton*, he would be to the Gentry *there*, what his Imitators *here*, are to him.

At *M'Crady*'s I formed an Intimacy with *Andrew Robertfon*, Efq ; who had been a Captain

tain in the *British* Service, which he quitted upon an honorable Connexion with a *Staten Island* young Lady of moſt exquiſite Beauty. The debonair and manly Appearance of young *Robertſon* attracted the Attention of the young Lady, which he improved by his Aſſiduity, and moſt excellent good Senſe. Altho' Miſs was ſtrongly fortified by Whiggiſm, yet ſhe was ultimately obliged to *ſuccumb* to the Proweſs of the young Officer, and about a Year ago became his Bride. This Gentleman is nearly related to the celebrated *Robertſon*, Author of the Hiſtory of the Reign of *Charles* the Fifth, Emperor of *Germany*, and under whoſe plaſtic Hand he received the Rudiments of that liberal Education, which ſo eminently diſtinguiſh and adorn his Character. From this Place I paid a Viſit to Col. *William Waſhington*, whom I found in Company with my old Preceptor the Rev. Mr. *Wilſon*. They were ſeated oppoſite to each other, about 5 Feet aſunder, ſeparated by two Wine Glaſſes and a Decanter of generous old *Madeira*. Upon my Entrance into the Room, after the firſt Gratulations and mutual Profeſſions of Friendſhip were over, a third Glaſs and another Decanter (as if by Enchantment) made their Appearance on the Table, and the Duumvirate was ſoon converted into a Triumvirate by the Addition of their humble Servant. Here gentle Reader, let me

whilſt

whilſt Friendſhip and the generous Glaſs ex-
pand my Heart, detain thee, with what Gratitude commands, in liſtening to my humble
Eulogy of *Waſhington*. 'Twas juſt after *Har-
mer*'s Defeat that theſe Thoughts occurred.

> Young Waſhington a former Friend in Need,
> I view him mounted on his gen'rous Steed ;
> The Foe he views with circumſpective Care,
> Cries Havoc ! and lets ſlip the Dogs of War :
> His ſmoking Horſes at their utmoſt Speed
> He laſhes on and urges o'er the Dead :
> Their Fetlocks run with Blood and when they bound,
> The Gore and gath'ring Duſt are daſh'd around.

Every Body is, or ought to be, acquainted
with the Brilliancies of this Gentleman as an
Officer and Soldier:—extraordinary as they are,
his mild engaging Virtues in the peaceful
Walks of Domeſtication, and in Society of
Friends, keep an equal Pace with his military
Talents, and draw from his admiring Coun-
trymen, the Plaudits of Sincerity.

> Raviſh'd with Wars and Danger's horrid Charms,
> He with impetuous Ardour flew to Arms :
> Soon as the rang'd Battalions came in Sight ⎞
> He felt fierce Joy and terrible Delight, ⎟
> And ſhudder'd with an Eagerneſs to fight. ⎠
> What Flames flew from his Eyes, when he from far
> View'd the four Brows, and murdering Jaws of War !

—OR THUS.—

> -rough in Battle
> As the firſt Romans when they went to War ;
> Yet after Victory more pitiful,
> Than all *their praying Virgins* left at Home.

DRYDEN.

Auguſt

August 6th. Returned to my Lodgings where I found Capt *Robertson* under Preparation for a Duel with Capt. *Sweetman*, an *English* Gentleman and Merchant.—I acted as a Mediator betwixt them, and happily terminated the Dispute to their mutual Satisfaction, by decreeing, that they both possessed indubitable Courage, which was often called into Action by their too punctilious Adherence to the military Character; for which their respective Countries had for many Centuries been so remarkable, and contributed equally with antient *Greece* and *Rome*, to give the historic Pen a just and full Employ—That inheriting these national Principles, what they had done, might be fairly traced up to the Source of an *Amor Pugnandi:*—That Capt. *Sweetman* had been too *precipitate* and Capt *Robertson* too *hasty:*—that they therefore make their reciprocal Concessions, and be at Peace; and that neither might infringe the Punctilios of military Etiquette, they should stand 10 Yards asunder, then advance to the Centre, make their Concessions at the same Instant, *protruding their dextral Hands, until they came into Contaction, as an Indication and Declaration* of a *Continuation of Pacification* : that they should then repair to the Hotel and take a *Compotation of a late Importation from the* Madeira *Plantation, in Corroboration of the* aforesaid *Pacification.*

Quicquid

Quicquid volumus facile credimus—The Duelliſt wiſhes to defend his Conduct. I will here
tranſcribe the Sentiments of a modern Author
upon the Subject of Duelling, which he ob-
ſerves, has in many Countries a Law againſt
it—but can never be prevented. The Law can
inflict no greater Penalty for any Breach of it
than Death ; which the Duelliſt contemns—
There are alſo ſome Cafes of Injury which
the Law cannot prevent, nor puniſh when
committed. Theſe muſt be redreſſed by the
Man who ſuffers, and by him ONLY. He is
prompted to do this by ſomething antecedent,
and ſuperior to all Law, and by a Deſire as
eager as Hunger or Luſt ; ſo that it is as eaſy
for Law to prevent or reſtrain the two latter,
as the former. Very luckily for us Occaſions
for the Gratification of this Paſſion occur but
ſeldom : and though a Man may be reſtrained
from a Duel by perſonal Fear, which is its
only Counteractor, there are very few In-
ſtances, perhaps none of its being prevented
by conſidering it as a Breach of Law. In
the Beginning of the laſt Century Duels were
ſo frequent, particularly in *France*, as to occaſion a ſevere Edict to prevent them—Indeed
by their Frequency, they were by Degrees improved into Combats of 2, 3, and ſometimes
more of a Side—In thoſe Days a French Nobleman was making up his Party to decide a
Quarrel

Quarrel with another Man of equal Rank ; it came to the Ears of the King, who fent to him one of the moft rifing Men at Court, with a Command to defift, affuring him of the ftrict Execution of the Edict in Cafe of Difobedience—Every one knows the Attachment of the *French* to their Soverign, but yet it proved weak when fet againft this all-powerful Paffion. The Nobleman not only refufed to obey the King, but actually engaged the Meffenger to be one of his Party.—The above feem to be the principal Reafons why Duelling has fo deep a Root in the Mind of Man —but there are others which come in Aid. The Defire of Superiority is of itfelf almoft fufficient to produce this great Effect.

Having fpent an agreeable Time among thefe gay and hofpitable Citizens, I took my Departure on Board the *Exchange* Schooner, the Property of Capt. *Robertfon*, and commanded by Capt. *Baine* ; her Deftination was to *St. Mary*'s River in Queft of Live-Oak.

A *Boftonian* of the Name of *James Foote*, had contracted with the Captain to work his Paffage from *Charlefton*, via *St. Mary's* to *New-York*. He appeared to be about 50 Years of Age, and extremely anxious to fee his Wife and five Children, whom he had left in *Bofton* about a Year before I faw him.

He

He had been detained by Sicknefs. On the
fecond Day of our Paffage, being as yet in a
State of Convalefcence, he expreffed in his
Words and Actions a fixed Melancholy, approaching to a State of Defperation. 'Twas
about 2 o'Clock in the Morning, when Mr.
Foote, to court the cooling Breeze, had feated
himfelf upon the Quarter Deck and received
an accidental Stroke from the Tiller on his
Head.—He rofe up and exclaimed, *My God,
My God, I cannot bear it all!* and quickly dif-
appeared.—I fincerely regret, that when I faw
him melancholy and defpondent, I had not
fpoken to him—I might probably have faid
Something to him, or done Something for
him, that might have footh'd the Anguifh of
his Soul, and by exciting Hope, have chafed
the gloomy Dæmon from his Breaft, and
caufed the poor defpairing Mortal yet to live.
This Voyage is ufually performed in about 4
Days, though through the Inadvertency, or
Ignorance of the Captain, we made it feven,
having over-ran our Reckoning, and inftead
of *St. Mary*'s failed a confiderable Diftance
up the *St. John*'s River in *Eaft-Florida*; when
to our great Aftonifhment we were hailed by
a *Spanifh* Officer, who authoritatively de-
manded of us, if we knew where we were?
We anfwer'd Yes; in *St. Mary*'s River—Gentlemen I can affure you, that you are miftaken;

L

you

you are now in the Dominions of *Spain*, and have rifqued the Forfeiture of your Veffel and Cargo, together with that of your Liberties. However you are welcome to depart—*St. Mary*'s River the Place of your Deftination, lies about 6 Leagues to the Eaftward of this. We thanked the Officer, inftantly put about, and in 5 Hours reached the Mouth of *St. Mary*'s, caft Anchor, and waited the Approach of a Pilot.—On our Entrance into this fine River, I obferved the Remains of an old Fort, compofed of *Portland* Stone, *Liverpool* Brick, and ftrong Cement, which, from its Expofure to the Sun and Wind, hath acquired a greater Durability than either the Brick or Stone. The Channel at the Mouth, which extends above an Hundred Yards in Width, is generally from 3 to 4 Fathom deep, and in no Part lefs than $2\frac{1}{2}$. We navigated a large Schooner deeply laden about 16 Miles up this River, and met with no Impediment whatever. A fimilar Diftance we run up the *St. John*'s, previous to our Arrival here—I think in Width and Depth they are nearly on a Par. The *St. Mary*'s is navigable for Sloops &c. about 60 Miles—Boats may proceed on as far as the Lake which feeds this Stream.—It is about 8 Miles long and 3 Miles wide, fituate in the Centre of a very extenfive Swamp, and diftant about 150 Miles from the Ocean. A

fmall

ſmall Town of the ſame Name with the River, now in the early Dawn of Infancy, lies
about 6 Miles up the Stream, where they have
a Fort garriſoned by a Company of Fœderal
Troops—The Evacuation of this Fort was
talked of when I left the Place, in Order to
ſtrengthen the Garriſon ſtationary on the
Oconee.

Diſappointed in having our Frieght of Live
Oak in Readineſs, we had much Leiſure on
our Hands, which Capt *Robertſon* and I reſolved to appropriate to the Exploration of
ſeveral Parts of *Eaſt-Florida*—For this Purpoſe we chartered a ſmall keel bottomed Boat,
and taking four Oars-men with us, proceeded along the inland Navigation, which leads
directly to the Neighbourhood of *St. Auguſ-
tine,* which however we were not permitted
to enter, and received repeated Intimations,
that a ſpeedy Return to *St. Mary*'s would ar-
gue the Height of *Prudence* in us, with
which the Captain and I were by no means
chargeable: For we had concerted no Plan
or plauſible Excuſe by which we might elude
the Vigilance or Jealouſy of the *Spaniſh*
Guarda Coſtas. *Robertſon* carried in his
Pocket, a Pencil and a ſmall Book, in which
he had made ſome rough Sketches of *Charleſton* and *St. Mary*'s. I wiſhed his Book and
Pencil

Pencil had been in his----------Bureau. Our Oars-men who were much alarmed, raifed a Blanket Sail, and plied the Oar with unremitting Affiduity, until we reached *St. Mary*'s, which exclufive of the Fort already mentioned, boafts two Stores, and a Tavern under the Direction of a Captain *Kearns*, who is a fenfible, intelligent Man, and furnifhes fuperior Accommodations than what are generally obtained in populous Cities. The River abounds in Scale and Shell-Fifh, all excellent in their Kind, and is often overfhadowed by the Flight of numerous Flocks of Swans, Geefe and Ducks. Thefe aquatic Productions are perennial, and from the Facility with which they are taken, render the Inhabitants near the Water, extremely averfe to agricultural Purfuits.

Having now explored the principal Parts of *Weft* and had a curfory View of *Eaft-Florida*, I am induced to hazzard my Opinion founded on Obfervation as to the former, and on Conjecture as to the latter. This I fhall do by a Quotation from *Guthrie*'s Grammar, which conveys my Sentiments. "The Air of both *Eaft* and *Weft-Florida* is pure and wholefome—The Size, Vigor, and Longevity of the *Floridian Indians*, in thefe Refpects, far exceed their more Southern Neighbours
the

the *Mexicans*:"—and I think Propriety may add, with few Exceptions, their Northern Neighbours too.—The Soil of the *Floridas*, is in general fandy, efpecially near the maritime Coafts, tho' far from being unfruitful.— It produces two Crops of *Indian* Corn a Year, and Garden Vegetables in great Perfection and Abundance. Without Cultivation the Orange and Lemon Trees attain a proper Size, and produce a large and highly flavoured Fruit. The interior Country is hilly, and on the Flats adjoining, extremely rich and fertile, producing fpontaneoufly, and in great Luxuriance, fimilar Fruits, Vegetables and Gums with *Georgia* and the *Carolinas*; as alfo Rice, Indigo, Ambergrife, Cochineal, Amethyfts, Lapis Lazuli, and other precious Stones; Copper, Quickfilver, Pit-Coal and Iron-Ore.

Pearls are found upon the Coafts—and Mahogany on the Southern Peninfula, but inferior in Size and Quality to that of *Jamaica*.—The Animal Creation here, are incredibly numerous.——What I have here advanced, muft be taken under fome Limitation; as in applies *in toto* and pofitively to *Eaft*, and only in Part to *Weft-Florida*.

Milton's Ode on *May* Morning, often occured to my Recollection, whilft traverfing
thefe

thefe delightful Regions, dreffed out by the Hand of Nature, with Flowers felected from her Lap.

O D E .

—

Now the bright Morning Star, Day's Harbinger,
Comes dancing from the Eaft, and leads with her
The flow'ry May, who from her green Lap throws,
The yellow Cowflip, and the pale Prim-rofe.
Hail ! bounteous May that does infpire
Mirth and Youth and warm Defire ;
Woods and Groves are of thy Dreffing,
Hill and Dale doth boaft thy Bleffing :
Thus we falute *thee* with our early Song
And welcome *thee* and wifh *thee* long.

Here as I am on the extreme Southern Verge of the United States, and in a fimilar Latitude with the Place where I promifed to fubjoin a Catalogue of medicinal Plants, Herbs, &c. I will attempt a Compliance.

WHITE WALNUT. *Juglans alba.* The *Creeks* make a ftrong Decoction from the Bark of this Tree, and ufe it both as a Cathartic and a Dye. In the former, they dulcify it with a little Honey, or the Syrup from the Sugar-Maple—It is very draftic in its Operation, and therefore adminiftered with great Caution.

BLACK POPLAR. *Populus nigra.* Large Potions of a Decoction from the Bark of this Tree, efpecially the Root, is a fovereign Antidote

tidote to the Bite of the *Rattle-Snake* and other Serpents—I was informed of this by General *Clarke*, whilſt in *Kentuckey*, who had ſeen its ſalutary Effects on five different Soldiers under his Command. The conſtant Uſe the *Indians* make of it on ſimilar Occaſions, corroborates the General's Aſſertion.

DOGWOOD. *Cornus Florida*. The pulverized Bark of this Tree, is cooling, drying, aſtringent and ſtomachic, and appropriated to ſimilar Purpoſes among the *Creeks* that *Jeſuits* Bark is among us, and for which it is a moſt excellent Subſtitute.

T H E CASSINE is a low umbrageous Tree: the Flower of which is patent, divided into five ſuboval, obtuſe Segments larger than the Cup; the Fruit is a roundiſh Berry with three Cells, containing ſolitary ſuboval Seeds—'Tis from the Leaves of this Tree, which are ſerrated and terminating in a Point, the *Creeks* make their *Black Drink*, of which they ſwallow copious Draughts, whenever they convene in their Square or Hot-Houſe, and which holding themſelves erect, they as copiouſly regurgitate. I am unacquainted with its medicinal Virtues, if it has any.—It is uſed by the *Spaniards* as a Tea and has a ſuperior Flavour to the *Green*, *Bohea*, or *Souchong*.

SASSA-

SASSAFRAS. *Laurus Saffafras.* A yellow odoriferous Wood, of a brifk, aromatic Scent, fomewhat refembling *Fennel*; being the Produce of a Tree, of which there are whole Forefts growing in the *Floridas*, as well as in this State. The principal Virtue lies in the Bark, which warms, dries, rarifies, attenuates, attracts and promotes Sweats and Urine. The *Indians* decoct and ufe it in all venerial Complaints, and I am told with great Succefs.

ELDER. *Sambucus nigra.* The *Creeks* decorticate the Stalk, and ufe the Bark in pectoral Decoctions. Sir *William Temple* extols it as a Medicine in dropfical Complaints. The *Creeks* exprefs the Juice, and ufe it as a Lotion in Burns, Scalds and fcabious Complaints.

SUMAC. *Rhus.* Applied to the firft Purpofe as mentioned of the *Elder*, as alfo to the Ufe of fmoking with *Tobacco*.

POKE. *Phytolacca decandra.* The *Creeks* collect the Berries whilft in a greenifh State, exprefs the Juice, and expofe it to the Sun until it coagulates, this they ufe in Plaifters over fchirrous Sores, or to extract Briars, Thorns, &c. from their Hands and Feet.— I have known it to be ufed in extracting the Claws or Roots of Cancers, &c.

ASH

ASH. *Fraxinus Americana.* A Decoction from the Root of prickly *Aſh*, is a good Purgative and Lotion in a confirmed Lues; and as ſuch is uſed by the *Creeks.*

JUNIPER. *Juniperus.* An Infuſion of the Berries of this Tree, in Water or Spirits, is ſtomachic, expels Wind, clears the Lungs, provokes the Menſes and removes Obſtructions of the Viſcera.

LOBELIA. With a Decoction of the Root of this Plant, the *Creeks* cure the Venerial Diſeaſe in every Stage. It uſually grows in Meadows, and on the fat low-Grounds of Rivers, Creeks, &c. It has a beauteous crimſon monopetalous Flower, and in Property is ſomewhat tingent. The Fruit is an oval Capſule, containing a great Number of very ſmall Seeds. The Decoction is uſually dulcified with Honey, which is a great Apperient. The Operation is by Stool, Urine, Sweat and Expectoration, all in a conſtant, though moderate Degree. Vide *Buchan* on a confirmed Lues, from the Beginning of Page 598 to the end of the Page following.

SERPENTARIA *Virginiana*, is an alexipharmic and ſovereign Remedy or Antidote againſt the Bite of the *Rattle-Snake.*—The different ſpecies of *Serpentaria* or *Snake root,*

 are

are univerfally known throughout the United States, by all Ranks of People. The Kind I allude to, is what is popularly called *Rattle-Snake* Root, which from its ftrong aromatic Smell, the *Rattle-Snake* will never approach, and is accordingly ufed by the *Indians* to banifh *that* and other Serpents from their Lodgments.

VALERIAN, *Valeriana Sylveftris, Ex Verbo valere.* It is warm and aromatic, but fomewhat fœtid in its Scent. The *Indians* ufe it in nervous Diforders. Its Efficacy as a Sudorific, is fupported by the Teftimony of both antient and modern Practice.

ANGELICA. *Angelica Sylveftris.* Is ufed as a Luxury in Smoking and Chewing.

ANATA. Is a Shrub of about five Feet high, bearing a red Flower, which the *Creeks* infufe in Water or decoct. With this Infu-fion or Decoction, they dye their Leggens, Moccafons, Feathers, Belts, and other or-namental Parts of Drefs.

The *Seminolies* who are connected with the *Creeks*, are faid, though more unpolifhed in their Manners, to have a greater Know-ledge in Botany, than their more Northern or Weftern Brethren.

Sept,

Sept.—Weighed Anchor, left *St. Mary's*, entered the Gulph Stream, and after a Paffage of Thirteen Days, reached the City of *New-York*; where, and in its Vicinage I continued about a Fortnight, experiencing Nothing more than common Civility from the Citizens.—The City of *New-York* is fituate on *Manhatan Ifland*; being a large handfome, and populous Place; where there is an excellent Harbour, furnifhed with commodious Quays and Ware-houfes, from whence numerous Ships and other Veffels are annually employed in its foreign Trade and Fifheries.

Paffed on in the New-York Packet Schooner to *Brunfwick*, the Metropolis of *New-Jerfey*, where I vifited Col. *White*, who refides in this Place. He is a brave, generous, old, Continental Officer, and made a confpicuous Figure on the Theatre of the laft *American* War with *Britain*. At this Place and in New-York, Meffieurs *Paine*, *Chevallie*, *Higbee*, *Laurence*, and *Griffin* Gentlemen from *Virginia*, rendered me polite Attention and Affiftance.——Gratitude fhall imprefs a long Remembrance of them on the Tablet of my Heart. A young *Englifhman* of the Name of *William Collier*, during my Indifpofition at New-York, dif-
played

played a Line of Conduct towards me, which does Honour to his Country and to human Nature.

This Indifpofition arofe from the Bite of a Ground Rattle Snake, on the Margin of *St. Mary's* River, in which I had been bathing. This little Reptile is about Fourteen Inches long, and about as thick as a Man's little Finger. It conceals itfelf in the Duft, and makes its malignant Stroke on the unwary and unfufpecting Paffenger, which is equally fatal with the Bite of the larger Rattle-Snake or Moccafon, and requires as fpeedy and powerful Antidotes to its baneful injections of ftrong and deadly Poifon.—— Providentially for me, it made its Puncture on the Cuticle of my great Toe, at the Adhefion of the Nail, which prevented a general Diffuffion of the Poifon into my Vital Parts.

As I paffed rapidly in the Stage through *Princeton* and *Trenton*, on my Way to *Philadelphia*, I muft wave a Defcription of the two former, and flightly touch upon the latter, which is a large, populous and extenfive Place, the Capitol and Emporium of *Pennfylvania*. In this charming City I continued ten Days, though unfortunately often confined

fined to my Room, from the Indifpofition laft mentioned. At Intervals of Eafe, I could not refrain from ftrolling through various Parts of the City, which for its Size and Regularity is unequalled by any other in the Union, and probably not furpaffed by any in Europe, as to the latter. Her Merchants are very wealthy, and her Citizens in general, from their Induftry and Frugality, raifed above the Frowns of Indigence, and many, though in humble, modeft Garb, far above a Mediocrity of Fortune.

Voltaire's Account of *Pennfylvania*, often occurred to my Recollection, whilft encircled by the humane unambitious Citizens of *Philadelphia*. In a Groupe of Quakers I particularly obferved an itenerant Preacher, whofe Afpect was a good Index of the Temper and Difpofition of Quakers in general.——I will attempt a Defcription of him, by fome Quotations from, and Interpolations of, Mr. *Dryden's* Parifh Prieft.

The PREACHER.

A Quaker Preacher, of the Pilgrim Train :
An awful, rev'rend, and religious Man.
His Eyes deffus'd a venerable Grace,
And Charity itfelf was in his Face.

Rich

Rich was his Soul, tho' his Attire was poor, ⎫
As God had cloth'd his own Ambaffador ; ⎬
For fuch, on Earth, his bleft Redeemer bore. ⎭
Refin'd himfelf to Soul, to curb the Senfe,
And made almoft a Sin of Abftinence.
Yet had his Afpect nothing of fevere,
But fuch a Face as promifed him fincere.
Nothing referv'd, or fullen was to fee; ⎫
But fweet Regards, and pleafing Sanctity, ⎬
Mild was his Accent ; and his Action free. ⎭
With Eloquence innate his Soul was arm'd ;
Tho' harfh the Precept, yet the Preacher charm'd.
He bore his great Commiffion in his Look :
But fweetly temper'd Awe and foften'd all be fpoke.
From his flight Stock be had fomewhat *to fpare,*
To feed the famifh'd, and to cloath the Bare :
And ever was at Hand without Requeft,
To ferve the Sick, and fuccour the Diftreft.
The Proud he tam'd, the Penitent he chear'd,
Nor to reprove the Rich Offender fear'd ;
His Preaching much, but more his Practice wrought,
(A living Sermon of the Truth he Taught.)
With what he beg'd, his Brethren he reliev'd,
And gave the Charities himfelf receiv'd:
Gave, while he taught, and edify'd the more,
Becaufe he fhew'd by Proof, 'twas eafy to be poor.

In my Perambulations through *Philadel-*
phia, (whofe Police is moft excellent) I do
not recollect ever to have feen a Beggar, or
heard that Prophanity and Vulgarity of Ex-
preffion, fo common amongft the lower
Clafs

Claſs in all other populous Cities; but on the contrary, diſcovered all Ranks decently habited, with a Serenity of Countenance, mild Addreſs, and in Steady, though moderate Purſuit of their reſpective Vocations.

A minute Deſcription of this City is both foreign to my Purpoſe, and beyond my KEN. I ſhall therefore only convey my Sentiments in a few Lines of doggrel Verſe, on three Gentlemen who reſide in this Place, and from whom I have recieved Favors and Polite Attention.

———◆———

To HENRY KNOX, ESQ. Secretary at War.

To EDMUND RANDOLPH, *Eſq*. Attorney Gen.

To SAMUEL PLEASANTS, *Eſq*. Merchant.

———

GENTLEMEN,

FROM me this Letter you'll receive,
    Th' Offspring of Affection,
Whilſt I my higheſt Plaudits give
    To your wiſe Election:

For

For who as Secretary could
 In Competition vie
With Knox *the gen'rous, brave and good?*
 Pale Envy anſwers—I.

And who with Randolph *can Compare*
 In ſmooth *Oratory*
When e're he brightens up the Bar,
 With ſweet Mel in Ore.

There were two Men dame Candour ſaid,
 Who equall'd him I wis,
In Rome *and* Athens *once they plead,*
 Tully *and* Demoſtth'nes.

Who can a nobler Work narrate
 Than what Sam : Pleaſants *is*
I muſt recur to antient Date
 And quote Ariſtides.

Who th' Epithet of Juſt *acquir'd*
 From his Intrinſic Worth;
Like him ſhall Pleaſants *be admired*
 For Honor, Juſtice, *Truth—*

By which I'm regulated when,
 ('Tis no Offence I hope)
I ſay you are three worthy Men
 As e'cr obliged————

POPE.

JUAN eſt muy verdadero. The Critics Sneer I do not dread:—for I have this humble Conſolation, that all my Work as being merely bottomed in TRUTH, will be an Object far below the Dignity of Criticiſm.—Sweet *Belle* and *Beau*, I had it once in Contemplation, to have furniſhed out Amuſement for you,—but dame Nature, the Miſtreſs of fair Genius, gave a ſlap upon my CEREBEL, and bade me to deſiſt.--------Here, gentle Reader, as thou art tired, I will make a ſtand, and if thou wilt forgive, declare—

TU ERES UN BUEN AMIGO.

TRANSLATED.

GOD BLESS THE HAND WHO GIVES ME
BREAD.

John you are a damned fool

ERRATA.

Page 11 l. 8 for " Relations" read " Relatives."
13 l. 13 for " excited" read " excite"
14 l. 7 for " awart" read " await"
— l. 13 for " Traits" read " Tracts"
17 l. 1 for " pureless" read " peerless"
— l. 3 for " evinc'd" read " evince"
18 l. 14 for " materially" read " material"
24 l. 13 for " Bayone" read " Bayoue"
27 l. 17 for " endangered" read " endamaged"
— l. 18 for " oppofing" read " oppreffing"
39 l. 2 for " Monaftry" read " Monaftery"
40 l. 5 for " Mammomilt" read " Mammoneft"
— l. 10 for " will" read " well"
41 l. 3 for " to" read " of"
47 l. 10 for " Tenfacola" read " Penfacola"
— l. 19 for " impaired" read " repaired"
55 l. 26 for " Augur" read " Augre"
59 l. 19 for " burried" " read " buri'd"
61 l. 6 before " Tails of numerous" read " broad"
62 l. 12 for " Monoty" read " Monotony"
68 l. 29 for " Ockmulga" read " Ockmulgee"
76 l. 16 for " as" read " for"
— l. 3 for " Breaft" read " Beaft"
79 l. 17 After " tho' " read " as"
86 l. 25 for " Contaction" read " Contactation"
93 l. 25 for " in applies" read " it applies."

INDEX.

Adultery: among Creeks, 56–57
Agriculture: among Creeks, 62–64
Alabama River, 46
Alexandrian Bluffs, 36
Allegheny Mountains: Pope crosses, 12; mentioned, 34
Alligators: Pope observes, 42; bite off Billy Pig's toe, 54
Altamaha River, 68
Ambergrise, 93
Amelia County, Va., 34
America, 80
American Revolution: Pope in, xi–xii, 9; Col. Thruston in, 8; George Rogers Clark in, 19–20; Gen. Anthony Wayne in, 41; Major Fairlamb in, 41; Loyalists, 67; in Georgia, 75; Col. M——e in, 75–76; mentioned, 72. *See also* Loyalists
Americans: in Pensacola, 43
Amethysts, 93
Amherst County, Va.: Pope resides in, xi, xii, xiii, 79
Anabaptism, 38
Anata: cataloged, 98
Andrea, Don, 39–40
Angelica: cataloged, 98
Anspacher, 25
Apples, 44, 48
Aristides, 104
Artichokes, 8–9
Ash: cataloged, 97
Athens, Greece, 104

Atlantic Ocean, 80
Augusta, Ga.: Pope visits, xxii, 72–74; mentioned, 75, 83

Bacon, 26, 34
Baine, Capt.: commands *Exchange*, 88; mentioned, xxx, note 22. *See also* "Bean," Captain
Ball match: Indian, 49–51
Baltimore, Md.: merchants in New Orleans, 41
Bayou Chappaliere: Pope describes, 35
Bayou Pierre: Pope passes and describes, 30, 33; mentioned, 35
Bayou St. John: Pope travels on and describes, 24, 42; mentioned, 37
Beall, Mr., 18
"Bean," Captain, xxx, note 22. *See also* Baine, Capt.
Bear meat, 21–22, 26
Beaver skins, 68
Beech Island, 75
Beef, 43
Beeson Town, Pa.: Pope observes, 12
Beetles, 65
Berkeley County, Va.: Pope travels through, xv, 10–11
Besheare, Captain, 24
Billy Pig: Indian legend, xxii, 54
Black Dog, 64–65
Blue Ridge Mountains: Pope crosses, 7
Boston, Mass., 88
Bourbon Township, Ky.: Pope passes through, 18
Boyd and Ker: letter to, 51, 52
Brackenridge, Hugh Henry: Pope meets, xv–xvi; Pope describes, 14–17; marriage, xxix, note 11, 14–17; mentioned, x
Braddock, Gen. Edward: Pope passes his grave, 12
British: and Pensacola, 43; in American Revolution, 75; mentioned, 67
Broken Arrow: Pope at, 52–53; mentioned, 60
Broken Arrow, Little King of: aids Pope, 54; furnishes Pope with Creek vocabulary, 65
Brunswick, N.J.: Pope at, xxiv, 99
Buffalo, 26, 59
Bugg and Watkins, Messrs.: Pope observes plantation, 75
Bully, the, 64

Burns' poems: quoted, 78
Butler, Senator Pierce: Pope describes, xxiii; Pope accompanies, 81–82; mentioned, x
Butler, Samuel: Pope's use of, xiii, 17
Butter, 34

Caesar, 69
Call, Major: Pope visits, 69–70
Cane, 30
Capuchins, 39
Carey, James, xxv
Carolinas, 30, 93
Cassine: cataloged, 95
Catfish, 26
Catholicism: in New Orleans, 38–41
Cattle, 36, 49
Cemetery: in New Orleans, 39, 40–41
Chancellor of Castille: grants divorce dispensation, 40
Chapel, 43
Charles V, Emperor of Germany, 84
Charleston, S.C.: Pope visits, xxiii, 81–88; mentioned, xxx, note 22, 91
Chattahoochee River: stopped by Billy Pig, 54; mentioned, xxii, 53, 59, 67
Chevallie, "Messieur": assists Pope, 99
Cherokee Indians, 61
Chesterfield County, Va., xii
Chickasaw Bluffs: Pope at, 23, 24
Chickasaw Indians, 24
Choctaw Indians: visit Pope, 25–26
Church. *See* Anabaptism; Catholicism; Methodism; Presbyterianism; Protestants
City Coffee House (Savannah): Pope lodges there, 79
Clark, Enrique. *See* Clark, George Rogers
Clark, Gen. George Rogers: Pope visits, xvi, 19–20; sends Pope on tour, xx, xxi; mentioned, x, xxx, note 12, 95
Clark, Francis Eleanor: marries O'Fallon, xvii, 29; described, xxx, note 12
"Clarke, Miss." *See* Clark, Francis Eleanor
Clay, Ensign: Pope visits, 69–70
Clover, 36
Coal: in Floridas, 93

Cochineal: in Floridas, 93

Coker, William S.: on Panton, Leslie and Company, xviii–xix

Colic, 48

Collier, William: assists Pope, 99–100

Commerce: in New Orleans, 41; Indian, 44–45; at Mobile and Pensacola, 47; in New York City, 99

Coosa River: Pope visits McGillivray on, xix, 46

Copper: in Floridas, 93

Copper mines, 43

Corn: festival, 55; planting among Creeks, 62–63; Pope observes fields, 75, 77; in Floridas, 93; mentioned, 33, 47, 60

Coweta: Pope at, 52–53; mentioned, 60

Cowpens, Battle of: Pope at, xi

Craig, Mr.: boat wrecks, 23–24, 34; again encounters Pope, 27

Cranes, 23

Creek Indians: Pope leaves, 52; war with Seminoles, 53; Pope on language, 54; punishment for fornication and adultery, 56–58; burial ceremony, 58–59; tattooing among, 60; music among, 62; agriculture among, 62–64; vocabulary, 65–66; trade at Oconee, 70–71; use of medicinal plants, 94, 95, 96, 97, 98; mentioned, 55, 72

Creek Nation: Pope leaves, xxii; Pope in, xxx, note 20; trade with Pensacola, 44; Turvin in, 67; mentioned, 5, 72

Creole (Don Andrea), 22

Crocodiles, 42

Culpepper County, Va.: Pope visits, 6

Cusseta: Pope at, 53; mentioned, 60

Cygnets, 23

Danville, Ky.: Pope visits, vii, 18–19; merchants accompany Pope, 13

Darisoux, Mr., 65

Deer skins, 44

Demosthenes, 104

Devil: and Creek language, 54

Disease. *See* Illness

Divorce of Don Andrea, 39

Dixon, John: publishes Pope's *Tour*, xxv–xxvi; on "Decemviri," xxxi, note 24

Dogwood: cataloged, 95

Douglass, Collin: letter to, 51, 52

Dryden, John: Pope's use of, xiii; quoted, 85, 101–2
Ducks, 92
Duel: Pope prevents, xxiii
Dueling: Pope on, 86–88
Duval, William: Pope sells land to, xii, xxviii, note 7

East Florida: Pope explores, xxiv, 89–90, 91–92; mentioned, 5. *See also* Floridas
Ebenezer, Ga.: Pope at, xxii, 75
Elder: cataloged, 96
Ellis, Mr., 34
England, 21, 72
Exchange, schooner: Pope takes passage on, xxiii, xxiv, xxx, note 22, 88

Fairlamb, Major: Pope meets, 41–42
Federal Fort (near the Oconee): Pope at, 69–71
Filson, John, 19
Flax, 6
Flint River: Pope crosses, xxii; Pope encamps on, 67; mentioned, 68
Floridas: description of, 92–94; mentioned, 39. *See also* East Florida; Pensacola; St. Augustine; West Florida
Flour, 26, 34
Fooley, Thomas: accompanies Pope, described, 13–14; Pope sees again in Louisville, 20–21
Foote, James: Pope describes, 88–89
Fornication: among Creeks, 56
Foucher, Pedro: Pope dines with, xvii, 22
France: dueling in, 87–88
Frederick County, Va., 10
Fredericksburg, Va., 11
French: religion of, 38; mentioned, 21, 22
Fruits, 44
Furs: as trade commodity, 70

Gates, Gen. Horatio: Pope sees, xv, 11; mentioned, x
Gayoso de Lemós, Gov. Manuel: Pope dines with, xvii, 29; mentioned, x, 30
Geese, 92
Georgia: Pope in, xxii, 69–81; mentioned, xiv, 23, 30, 42, 63, 67, 93. *See also* Augusta; Ebenezer; Purisburg; St. Marys; Savannah; Washington

Germantown, Pa., 77
God: Creek word for, 54
Grand Gulph, 29
Grand-Pré, Carlos de: Pope dines with, xvii, 31; mentioned, x
Gray, David, 11
Greasy Bend. *See* Neuvo Madrid; New Madrid
Greene, Gen. Nathaniel, 77
Great Britain, 21, 72
Griffin, "Messieur": assists Pope, 99
Gulf Coast: health on, xviii
Gulf of Mexico, 35
Gulf Stream, 99
Guthrie's Grammar: quoted, 92–93

Habersham, Col. Joseph: Pope talks with, xxii, 79; mentioned, x
Havana, Cuba, xxi
Headache: McGillivray's, 48
Health: in Pensacola, 44
Hemp, 6, 47
Henry, Patrick: and Virginia Yazoo Company, xiv, xxix, note 10
Hickory trees, 46
Higbee, "Messieur": assists Pope, 99
Hobdy, John: invents machine, 6
Hogs, 49
Horses: Pope observes, 36; mentioned, 49
Hospital: in New Orleans, 39, 40
Howard, Mr.: buys cemetery, 41
Hudibras: quoted, xiii, 17
Hunter, Moses, 11

Illness: Pope experiences, xv; in Pensacola, xviii–xix; of McGillivray, 52. *See also* Colic; Headache; Health; Rattlesnake bite; Rheumatism; Yellow fever.
Indians: escort Pope, xix; Pope travels in territory, xix–xxii, 45–69; Pope records folk tradition among, xxii; Pope's fear of attack by, 22; and mosquitoes, 35; and alligators, 42; boundary, 46; ball match, 49–51; festival (busk), 55–56; assist Pope, 68–69; use of medicinal plants, 94, 95, 96, 97, 98; mentioned, 92–93. *See also*

Cherokee Indians; Chickasaw Indians; Choctaw Indians; Creek Indians; Ozark Indians; Seminole Indians
Indigo: Pope observes fields of, 77; in Floridas, 93; mentioned, 33
Irish, 25, 26
Iron ore: in Floridas, 93

Jamaica, 93
Jamestown, Battle of: Pope at, xi
Jesuits, 38
Jesuits Bark, 95
Judas Iscariot, 38
Juniper: cataloged, 97

Kearns, Capt., 92
Kentucky: Pope in, 18–21; mentioned, 5, 11, 17, 25, 38, 75, 95. *See also* Bourbon Township; Danville; Lexington Township; Limestone; Louisville; Washington Township
"Kentucky Boat," 13
Knox, Secretary of War Henry: Pope visits, xiv, xxiv; poem for, 103; mentioned, x, xxx, note 20

Lafayette, Marquis de: Pope serves under, xii
Langue la Graisse. *See* Neuvo Madrid
Lapis lazuli: in Floridas, 93
Las Casas, Luis de: on Pope's "intrigue," xxi
Laurel Hill: Pope at, 12
Laurence, "Messieur": assists Pope, 99
Lee, Gen. Charles, 11
Lemon trees, 93
Lexington Township, Ky.: Pope passes through, 18
Limestone, Ky.: Pope passes through, xvi, 18
Little Tallassee, 51
Live Oak. *See* Oak trees
Lobelia: cataloged, 97
Loftus' Bluffs: Pope observes, xvii, 34–35
London, England, 29, 45
Long Reach: Pope at, 35
Lord's Prayer: Pope attempts to teach, 71–72, 73
Louisiana: Pope in, 21–42; mentioned, 5. *See also* New Orleans

Louisville, Ky.: Pope visits, xvi, 19–21; mentioned, 22
Loyalists: in Georgia, 76; mentioned, 67
Lumber, 34
Lynch's Ferry, Battle at: Pope at, xi

M'Crady's Hotel (Charleston): Pope rooms at, xxiii, 82–83
McGillivray, Alexander: Pope visits, xix–xxii, 46–52; on
    Pope's letter to Wilcox, xx; mentioned, x, xxx, note 20,
    5, 65
McGillivray, Alexander (son of the Creek chief), 49
McGillivray, Elizabeth, 49
McIntosh, Gen. Lachlan: Pope visits, xxii, 79–81
Mahogany: in Floridas, 93
Manchester, Va.: Pope resides at, xii, xiii; mentioned, 51,
    52
Manhattan Island, 99
Martin, Lieut.: Pope visits, 69–70
Martinsburg, Va.: Pope visits, xv, 11
Maryland, 13. *See also* Baltimore
Medicinal plants: cataloged, 94–98
Methodism, 38
Mexicans, 93
Milton, John: Pope's use of, xiii; quoted, 93–94
Miró, Estevan: McGillivray writes, xx, xxi; on Pope's
    "intrigue," xxi; receives instructions concerning Pope,
    xxi; mentioned, 37
Mississippi River: Pope travels down, xvi, xvii, 21–36;
    Spanish posts on, xx; at New Orleans, 36–37; mentioned,
    41
Mobile, Ala.: prisoners in, 43; Pope on, 46–47; mentioned,
    42, 45, 71
Mobile Bay, 46
Mobile River, 46
Monastery, 39
Monongahela River: Pope travels, xv, 12–13; mentioned,
    10
M——e, Col.: Pope visits, 75–76
Morgan, Gen. Daniel: Pope visits, xv, 10; mentioned, x
Mosquitoes: Pope complains about, xvii, 35
Murphy, Patrick: punished by Creeks, 57
Muscovite ducks, 23
Music: among Creeks, 62
Mutton, 43

Natchez: Pope visits, xvii, 30–34; Pope's alleged intrigue at, xx; commandant at to be reprimanded, xxi; governor of, 28; mentioned, xvii, 27, 28, 29, 35

Negroes: and alligators, 42; prisoners, 42–43; at McGillivray's plantation, 49; slaves, Pope observes, 78; mentioned, 77

Neuvo Madrid: Pope at, 21–23; mentioned, 27, 35. *See also* New Madrid

New Jersey: Pope in, 99–100. *See also* Brunswick; Princeton; Trenton

New Madrid: Pope visits, xvii. *See also* Neuvo Madrid

New Orleans: Pope visits, xvii–xviii; Pope's alleged intrigue at, xx; commandant at to be reprimanded, xxi; Pope at, 36–42; mentioned, 23, 27, 35

New Providence Island: salt works on, xviii, 44–45

New Town: Pope visits, 7

New York: Pope in, xxiv, 99; merchants in New Orleans, 41; McGillivray in, 51; mentioned, xxx, note 22, 28, 52, 88

Nile River, 42

Nuns, 39

Oak trees, 46, 88, 91

Ocmulgee River: Pope crosses, xxii, 68

Oconee River: Pope crosses, xxii, 69; mentioned, 68, 91

O'Fallon, James: and Yazoo Company, xvii; to lead expedition against Spanish, xxi; describes Francis Eleanor Clark, xxx, note 12; Pope on, 29

Ogeechee River, xxii, 71

Ohio River: Pope travels down, xvi, 18, 21; mentioned, 10, 22

O'Neill, Governor Arturo: Pope visits, xviii, 44; on health in Pensacola, xviii; mentioned, x

Opossum, 69

Orange trees, 93

Ozark Indians: Pope observes, 26

Ozark River, 26

Paine, "Messieur": assists Pope, 99

Panton, Leslie and Company: Pope on xviii–xix, 44–45

Pearls: in Floridas, 93

Peltry, 75

Pennsylvania: Pope in, 100–103; mentioned, 26. *See also* Germantown; Laurel Hill; Philadelphia; Pittsburgh; Washington County

Pennsylvania Mercury: on H. H. Brackenridge's marriage, xxix, note 11.

Pensacola: health in, xviii; Pope visits, xviii–xix, 43–45; Pope's alleged intrigue at, xx; commandant at to be reprimanded, xxi; governor of, 21–22; mentioned, 42, 46, 47, 58, 66, 71, 73

Philadelphia, Pa.: Pope in, xxv, 100–103; Sabina Wolfe sent to, 15–16; merchants in New Orleans, 41; mentioned, xv, 77

Pine trees: Pope observes, 34; mentioned, 46

Pittsburgh, Pa.: Pope at, xv–xvi, 13, 14–18; boats from, 26

Pittsburgh *Gazette:* published Pope's poem, xvi, 16–17

Pleasants, Samuel: poem dedicated to, xxv, 103–4

Point Coupée: Pope observes, xvii, 36

Poke: cataloged, 96

Pope, Alexander (author): Pope's use of, xiii; on moral behavior, xviii; quoted, 40

Pope, Alexander D.: *Tour*, dedicated to, xxv

Pope, Anne: *Tour*, dedicated to, xxv

Pope, Col. John: *Tour*, x–xi, xiv, xvi, xxv–xxvii; biographical sketch, xi–xiii; purpose of trip, xiii–xiv; summary of tour, xiv–xxv; intrigue by, xx–xxi; author of "Decemviri," xxxi, note 24; tour in Virginia, 5–12; in Pennsylvania, 12–18; writes poem about Brackenridge, 16–17; in Kentucky, 18–21; trip down the Mississippi River, 21–36; at New Orleans, 36–42; in West Florida, 43–45; in Indian country, 45–69; in Georgia, 69–81; in South Carolina, 81–88; travels to St. Marys and vicinity, 88–94; catalogs medicinal plants, 94–98; passage to New York, 99; bitten by rattlesnake, 100; travels from New York City to Philadelphia, 99–103

Pope, Lucinda C.: *Tour*, dedicated to, xxv

Poplar, black: cataloged, 94–95; mentioned, 46

Pork, 43

Potatoes, 60

Presbyterianism, 38

Primate of Spain: grants divorce dispensation, 40

Princeton, N.J.: Pope passes through, xxiv, 100
Prisoners: described, 42–43
Protestants: cemetery for, 41
Purisburg, Ga.: Pope passes by, xxii, 77

Quakers: Pope on, 101–2
Quevedo y Villegas, Francisco Gomez de: quoted, 18
Quicksilver: in Floridas, 93

Randolph, Attorney General Edmund: poem dedicated to, xxv, 103–4
Rapidan River: Pope crosses, 5
Rattlesnake: cure for bite, 95, 97–98; bites Pope, 100
Rattlesnake root: Pope on, 97–98
Red River: Pope observes, 35
Redstone: Pope arrives at, xv, 12; mentioned, 13
Revolution, American. *See* American Revolution
Rheumatism: Pope "contracts," 5; recurs, 14; mentioned, xv
Rice: Pope observes fields of, 77; in Floridas, 93; mentioned, 33, 60
Richmond, Va., ix, x, xii, xiii, xiv, xv, xxv, 5, 51, 52
Richmond County, Va., xii
Robertson, Capt. Andrew: Pope describes, 83–84; duel, 86; owns *Exchange*, 88; and Pope explore East Florida, 91–92
Rockfish Gap, Battle at: Pope at, xi
Rome, Italy, 104
Roosevelt, Theodore: quoted, xiii
Ross, Captain: Pope sails on his ship, 81; mentioned, xxx, note 21
Ross, David: and Virginia Yazoo Company, xiv
Rudolph, Capt.: Pope visits, 69–70
Rum: and Indians, 46
Rutherford, Robert: Pope meets, 11

St. Augustine: Pope approaches, xxiv; Turvin flees to, 67; mentioned, 91
St. Francis River, 26
St. John, Bayou. *See* Bayou St. John
St. John's River: Pope travels, xxiii, 89–90

St. Marks, 45, 66, 67, 71
St. Mary's: Pope's trip to, xxiii–xxiv, 88–94, 99; mentioned, xxx, note 22, 52
St. Mary's River: Pope travels to, 88–94; mentioned, 68, 81, 100
St. Patrick, 25
Salt, 26, 44
Sassafras: cataloged, 96
Savannah, Ga.: Pope visits, xxii, 78–81; mentioned, 75, 77, 83
Savannah River: Pope travels down, xxii, 74–79; bridge over, 74
Scotland, 51, 79
Scott, Gen., 19
Seminole Indians: knowledge of botany, 98; mentioned, 53
Senetahawgo: harangues Indians, 60–62
Serpentaria: cataloged, 97–98
Shenandoah River: navigation of, 7
Shepherd, Col.: accompanies Pope, 12
Shepherd's Town, Va.: Pope visits, xv, 11
Sickness. *See* Illness
Slaves. *See* Negroes
Smellfungus, 21
Smelt & Williamson, Messrs., 74
Smoke-House (boat): Pope travels on, 23
South Carolina: Pope in, 81–88. *See also* Carolinas; Charleston
Spanish: turn Pope back on St. John's River, xxiii–xxiv, 89–90; described, 31–33; religion of, 38; prisoners, 42–43; in West Florida, 43–45
Spanish king, 28, 41
Spanish soldier: Pope on, xviii
Stafford County, Va., 29
Staten Island, N.Y., 84
Stephen, Gen. Adam: Pope visits, xv, 11; mentioned, x
Sterne, Mr., 20–21
Sumac: use by Creeks, 63; cataloged, 96
Swaine, Capt., 27
Swans, 92
Sweetman, Capt.: duel, 86
Swinburne, Mr.: quoted, 31–33

Tallapoosa River, 46
Tarantula, 62
Tarleton, Banastre, 10
Tattooing: among Creeks, 60
Taverns: at Pensacola, 43; mentioned, 92
Telfair, Governor Edward: Pope visits, xxii; mentioned, x
Telfair, William: misnamed by Pope, xxii; Pope visits, 74
Temple, Sir William: on use of elder, 96
Tennessee River, xiv
Thieves: Pope's problem with, xv, 9–10
Thomas, schooner: Pope takes passage on, xxii, xxx, note 21
Thornton, Col. John: nurses Pope to health, 6
Thornton, William: invents water mill, 6
Thruston, Col. G. M.: Pope visits, 7, 8
Tobacco: planting among Creeks, 63; mentioned, 23, 26, 27, 33–34, 47, 74–75, 96
Toledo, Archbishop of: grants divorce dispensation, 39–40
Tombigbee River, 46
Tories. *See* Loyalists
Trenton, N.J.: Pope passes through, xxiv, 100
Tully, 104
Turtle eggs, 69
Turvin, John: accompanies Pope, 67–73

United States: citizens of, 28, 35; southern boundary, 81
University of Virginia, x

Valerian: cataloged, 98
Venereal disease: cure for, 96, 97
Venison, 25, 44
Verulam, Lord, 20–21
Violin: among Creeks, 62
Virginia: Pope passes through, 5–12; soil in, 73; mentioned, iv, 18, 25, 29, 30, 99. See also Amelia County; Amherst County; Berkeley County; Chesterfield County; Culpepper County; Frederick County; Fredericksburg; Manchester; Martinsburg; Richmond; Richmond County; Shepherd's Town; Stafford County; Williamsburg; Winchester
Virginia, Assembly of: votes premium for John Hobdy, 6
Virginia, state of: authorizes Pope to attack Spanish, xx

Virginia Gazette and Public Advertiser, Richmond, xxv
Virginia Gazette & Richmond Daily Advertiser: carries
    notice of *Tour* publication, xxv
Virginia Senate, 11
Virginia Yazoo Company: Pope as agent of, xiv, xxix, note
    10
Voltaire, François Marie Arouet de: Pope's use of, xiii, 101

Walnut, white: cataloged, 94; mentioned, 46
Walnut Hills: as Gayoso's destination, xvii; Pope observes,
    28; mentioned, 29
Washington, Charles: Pope visits, xv, 11; mentioned, x
Washington, George: visits Charleston, xxiii, 83; and Mc-
    Gillivray, 51; mentioned, 12, 61
Washington, Col. William: Pope visits, xxiii, 84–85
Washington, Ga.: Pope visits, xxii, 71
Washington County, Pa., 14
Washington Township, Ky.: Pope passes through, 18
Water moccasin, 100
Wayne, Gen. Anthony: in American Revolution, 41; Pope
    has message for, 42; mentioned, 75
Welch, 25
Welch, John: steals Pope's horse, 9–10
West Florida: Pope in, 43–45; mentioned, 5, 92
West Indies, 49
Wheat, 6
White, Col.: Pope visits, 99
Wilcox, Tairux: Pope writes, xx; mentioned, xxi
Wilkinson, Gen. James, 19, 27
Williamsburg, xxv
Wilson, Rev. Mr.: Pope visits, 84–85
Winchester, Va.: Pope visits, xv, 9–10; mentioned, 7
Wine: and Indians, 46
Wolfe, Mr.: Brackenridge visits, 14–15
Wolfe, Sabina: marriage to Brackenridge, xvi, 14–17
Woodward, Charles L.: reprinted Pope's *Tour*, xxvi

Yazoo Company: and O'Fallon, 29
Yazoo River, xvii, 28
Yellow fever: on Gulf Coast, xviii
Yorktown, Battle of: Pope at, xii

Zane, Col. Isaac: Pope visits, 7–8; mentioned, x